Historic FLORIDA CHURCHES

Historic
FLORIDA
CHURCHES

JOY SHEFFIELD HARRIS

THE
History
PRESS

Published by The History Press
Charleston, SC
www.historypress.com

First published 2024

Manufactured in the United States

ISBN 9781467155724

Library of Congress Control Number: 2023949156

Notice: The information in this book is true and complete to the best of our knowledge. It is offered without guarantee on the part of the author or The History Press. The author and The History Press disclaim all liability in connection with the use of this book.

To my husband, Jack.

CONTENTS

ACKNOWLEDGEMENTS

With gratefulness and appreciation, thank you to the following people for the encouragement and support they gave me while I was researching and writing *Historic Florida Churches*:

Joe Gartrell, acquisitions editor, and Zoe Ames, copyeditor, at The History Press.

Kelly Smith for her meticulous editing of *Historic Florida Churches*.

Rick Bringger and other classmates from Rutherford High School along with social media friends who shared with me their church stories and photos.

My friends Lisa Tamargo, Ellen Nafe, Charles and LeAnn Knight, Peter Borg, Aaron Jacobson and George Carl and my cousin Lisa Kalmbach.

My brother Dennis and his wife, Laurelyn Sheffield, who gave me one of my favorite Bibles when I was young.

My brother Pat; his wife, Carolyn Sheffield; and their daughter, Hannah Abraham, for sharing their church stories and photos with me.

My husband, Jack, and our son, Jackson.

THE MYSTERY OF HISTORY

Exploring Florida's History Through Churches

No mission station is equipped until there is a house of prayer; a place where
God's name is recorded, and where his people meet to worship.
—*John Cole Ley*

W ho built that church?" Driving along the rural roads of Florida, you may have seen the steeple of a tiny church as you approach the once-bustling main street of what seems like a long-forgotten town. As you slow down to look, the beauty of the past comes alive through these revered churches, often at the center of town—and life—as the state took hold and started to grow two hundred years ago. This is the story of what my husband, Jack, and I discovered during our journey through the state. It all started with one little church sitting alongside a busy highway in rural Florida, the First Baptist Church of Citra in Marion County. It sparked a curiosity to know more about these beautiful old churches, launching our two-year expedition searching the highways and byways along with the backroads, crossroads and isolated dirt roads for these treasured structures. Churches such as the First Baptist Church of Citra are scattered throughout Florida and bring charm and spiritual guidance to both urban and rural areas.

The town of Citra was settled in the early 1880s, and not long after, the First Baptist Church of Citra was built in 1893. A Victorian influence on this Carpenter Gothic–style church gives it a unique look, with its intricate details including rose windows set on either side of the square base of an octagonal belfry. But the town of Citra is also home to an even older church, the Citra First United Methodist Church or Citra Methodist Episcopal Church. Located a few blocks southwest of the Baptist church is a frame vernacular meetinghouse built in 1881 through the efforts of a circuit-riding preacher and a generous community. According to one source, the original bell still rings every Sunday.

Churches are more than places of worship. They are hubs that draw people together for spiritual guidance but also for education and other purposes. I remember sitting with my father on the steps of a country church in Steinhatchee as he told me the story of a young man from Vernon who set fire to his church, which also served as a school in the 1930s. It was a tragic day to lose such an important building that met the needs of the locals in so many ways. These historic structures are sources of inspiration as we strive to make our world a better place for those who live among us and for those who follow.

A simple Internet search led to a two-year study of Florida churches through movies, books, parks, museums, libraries and interviews. Information found on the National Register of Historic Places, the State Archives of Florida, Florida Memory and the Florida Division of Historical Resources, including the Florida Historical Marker Program—as well as church blogs and websites—provided so many answers, but not all. On our journey, Jack and I photographed more than two hundred old Florida churches, and the past beauty of many can be seen on postcards and photographs found in the Florida Archives. *Historic Florida Churches* serves as a guide to areas that are home to Florida's historic churches, from the oldest Catholic parish in the United States to the place where Billy Graham found inspiration to preach. Florida's history encompasses a religious diversity reflected in architectural vestiges of early churches that show the changing style as the state went from Native American villages to early Spanish settlements to English plantations and, later, poverty-stricken communities, followed by remnants left from wealthy northern visitors. Searching for the origins of these churches while driving from town to town brought more questions, and the answers go back centuries. The search for a meaningful life as expressed through man-made structures—whether Stonehenge in England with its massive trilithons, the pyramids of Egypt or a tiny chapel built in Florida—offers a chance to reflect on those who came before us and what this life means.

From the Ice Age to the Stone Age to the Bronze Age to the Iron Age, mankind has searched for more than food and shelter. Florida Paleo-Indians crossed a land bridge where the Bering Sea is now and migrated southeast, eventually ending up in Florida more than twelve thousand years ago. As

On their honeymoon in 1986, Joy and Jack Harris stopped by the approximately five-thousand-year-old Stonehenge in Wiltshire, England, on Salisbury Plain southwest of London. *Author's collection, 1986.*

the Ice Age thawed, others followed for thousands of years, which led to the Archaic culture and the construction of hundreds of temple mounds, used for ceremonial and religious purposes, as well as kitchen middens, some of which can still be seen today. These ancient sites give a glimpse into some of the religious practices of early inhabitants up to the 1500s and the Spanish mission period. Historic mounds appear throughout the state, from the burial mounds at Fort Walton Beach Temple Mound to Crystal River Archaeological State Park. The Portavant Temple Mound at Emerson Point Preserve in Palmetto along with the historical timeline up to the 1890s at Selby Gardens' Historic Spanish Point in Osprey give a glimpse of ancient middens. The Tallahassee area is home to Lake Jackson Mounds Archaeological State Park, featuring six earthen temple mounds and a re-created Apalachee village at Mission San Luis.

The establishment of Christianity and the events of the Bible paint a picture of the struggle to live a godly life, from the writing of the Ten Commandments and the ancient temples of the Old Testament to the New Testament, which details how a new life can be found through Jesus Christ, the foundation of Christianity. The Christian church started with the Holy Spirit–filled Apostles of Christ after the ascension of Christ to heaven. Christian worship based on the life and teachings of Jesus Christ began as people met in homes to share this new beginning. Local churches were established to preach, teach and guide those seeking the word of God.

The practice of religion in the safety of shelter has led to some of the most captivating architecture in the world. Dura Europos, a former Roman fortress city, is home to what's left of one of the oldest synagogues in the world, as well as the oldest Christian house-church discovered to date. Christians practiced their religion secretly in homes until Christianity was declared legal. Over time, religious conflicts ensued, and houses of worship were destroyed, only to be rebuilt in peace when Roman emperor Constantine embraced Christianity in 313 BC. Later, early Roman churches were built directly over some of those ancient church-homes.

Around AD 400, the books of the Bible were selected and compiled. When searching for biblical history, the story of how the Bible came to be is explained at the Museum of the Bible (MOB) in Washington, D.C. MOB is not only a Christian initiative but also an educational, entertaining and immersive way to learn about the history of the Bible. The New Testament was written around the same time the Roman Colosseum was constructed. This oval amphitheater in the center of Rome still stands today, as do the teachings of the Bible. One is antiquated and open for tours, the other a spiritual guidepost.

For hundreds of years, there was only one church and no denominations. Beginning in AD 1054, the Christian Church was divided into two main branches. This event, known as the Great Schism, occurred when the Western Roman Catholic Church broke away from the Eastern Orthodox Christian Church. The Protestant Reformation brought about hundreds of denominations that split from the Roman Catholic Church, starting with the Lutheran Church. A dozen denominations split from the Lutheran Church, including the Presbyterian Church. The Church of England was established in Europe. Groups would splinter off, such as the Methodists and the Anabaptists, which were divided among the Amish, the Mennonites and the Quakers.

From the majestic beauty of the Gothic Notre Dame Cathedral in Paris to St. Peter's Basilica in Rome, churches have long been a haven for the lonely, the weary, the sick and the sinner. They are part of a nation's foundation. Construction on Notre Dame began in 1163 and took almost two hundred years to complete. In 1506, construction was begun on St. Peter's Basilica, built on the site of a fourth-century church, which took about 120 years

Jack and Joy with their son, Jackson, at the Gothic cathedral Notre Dame de Paris. Historic churches have long been of interest to the Harris family. *Author's collection, 2011.*

to complete. While these magnificent structures were being built across the Atlantic, in Florida the peninsula's religious-political leaders were emerging among the various Indigenous tribes who inhabited the state.

One notable event that led to the rapid spread of Christianity happened in 1215 when the Magna Carta, protecting religious freedom, was signed at Runnymede in England. Another in 1456, the invention of the printing press by movable type, led to the printing of the Gutenberg Bible. It wasn't until the 1600s that the King James version of an English Bible was available to the public, and today there are thousands of translations.

In 1492, Christopher Columbus set sail from Spain across the Atlantic in search of gold, spices and a shorter route to India. Spanish and French soldiers, priests and friars came to the Americas with a zealous desire to spread Christianity around the world. Others came in search of religious freedom. Widespread European exploration, colonization and conflicts in the New World began. A Spanish influence is still found throughout the state, which makes Florida an eclectic showcase of architecturally significant churches. From the oldest church built in the state, the Cathedral Basilica of St. Augustine, to the ancient Spanish Monastery of St. Bernard de Clairvaux, built in AD 1141 and transported piece by piece to Miami in 1964, the Spanish influence is reflected beautifully. Religion and faith in God have long been a source of inspiration throughout the world. The Florida Capitol is one of the few statehouses that has a chapel, the Heritage Chapel. In 2006, Florida made its official state motto "In God We Trust."

Introduction

GONE BUT NOT FORGOTTEN

Suppose we do build a church in a place which becomes deserted, so that the church building remains as the only evidence of past zeal and enterprise, has the labor been wasted? Was the effort a mistake?
—The Right Reverend Edwin Gardner Weed, Episcopal bishop of Florida

An old-fashioned sign, "Our Churches Welcome You," alongside a once-rural road evokes a time of pioneer days and community building, reminiscent of the days when open windows welcomed a refreshing breeze and church doors were always left unlocked. The E.E. Cummings poem "I Am a Little Church" is a reminder of the simple beauty of these now-historic gems, as the first line reads: "I am a little church (no great cathedral)."

Those who came before us found a way to create a church out of God's natural resources. Built to serve as inspiration, today these churches are a reminder of their dedication and hard work to bring a purposeful building to the community. At times, the church was the first building constructed in the town. Whether a multipurpose meetinghouse serving as a church on Sundays and public school during the week or a beautiful and graceful cathedral in the city, the buildings don't last forever, but the photographs, memories and purpose remain. History lingers and gives us hope as we continue to search for greater meaning in these old Florida churches. The First Baptist Church of Gainesville, built in the late 1880s, was left with only a bell tower due to natural disasters, and later the bell tower was demolished.

The First Baptist Church of Gainesville, built in the late 1800s, suffered from tornado and then fire damage. The sanctuary was destroyed in the 1950s, and demolition of the bell tower occurred in 1965. Photos circa 1900 (*this page, top*), circa 1950 (*this page, bottom*) and 1965 (*opposite*). *Courtesy of the State Archives of Florida.*

Many areas went from pioneer settlements to bustling steamboat and railway towns, as reflected in the charming Main Street communities featured in Florida tourism brochures. Some historic churches appear largely unchanged. Some have been moved, some removed, others remodeled and still others extensively modified—and some are lost, only to be found in photographs. From the beauty of Carpenter Gothic to the rustic simplicity of a country church, shadows of the past come alive. Looking at old Florida churches in their natural setting gives more insight into the history, work and experiences of that era. There is something spiritual about seeing a small community church nestled within the sylvan countryside of rural Florida. That is precisely what was meant to happen when many churches were constructed in Florida.

Many of Florida's fascinating churches stand today as monuments to the strength of the community through a continued effort to maintain, repair and restore these historic gems dedicated to the glory of God. The ringing of the church bell still beckons in some towns, while honeybees set up their own communities in the belfries of others. We encountered a variety of other creatures along the way while searching for these historic gems—from a friendly stray dog to a group of cows leisurely crossing the road as their owners were frantically trying to mend the fence and corral them back to their pasture. The most unusual sight was the camels we saw grazing alongside a rural road near Mikesville Presbyterian Church in Columbia County. Some churches have a story beyond their beauty or historical significance, while others stand alone showcasing their grace, both physical and spiritual. While searching for an old wooden church in a charming Lake County neighborhood, we were surprised to see the beautiful, ornate First Presbyterian Church of Eustis sitting quietly on the corner. Some of these churches are famous, with stories created around them, while others are beautiful in their simplicity. One can almost see history blossom.

Florida's natural history is as picturesque as its spiritual history and only adds to the beauty of these hidden gems. Ancestors of Native Americans crossed the Bering Strait in search of a new home as they slowly migrated south. The riverbeds of Florida have protected prehistoric evidence of settlements across the state. Hidden in the soil are tools, fabric and other remains of ancient Florida settlements. Florida has long been a haven for those seeking a better life. Before sugar mills and turpentine stills, cracker homes and community churches, our more recent pioneer settlers met in homes, or beneath brush arbors, and often shared the spaces with different faiths throughout the day to worship. The need for churches was growing along with the population. Hard times were expected when forging a new frontier, and a place to rest and refresh the soul was vital. For some, it was a simple haven from the swampland. Enormous effort went into the building of a church.

Today, natives as well as seasonal visitors are at home in the Sunshine State. The five flags flown over Florida—Spain, France, Great Britain, the United States and the Confederate States of America—not only represent the state's rich history but also encompass a religious diversity that led to wars between Spain, France, England and what was to become the United

Bethel African Methodist Episcopal Church, Tallahassee, built in the late 1800s, served the community until 1982. The stained-glass windows were restored and placed in the new building. Photo circa 1888. *Courtesy of the State Archives of Florida.*

States, as well as the Civil War. Some of these churches tell the story of a post–Civil War Florida as it struggled to reestablish itself as a place of welcome for all.

The founding of the first Florida African Methodist Episcopal (AME) church in 1865 ushered in a new denomination that hoped to escape the racial discrimination so common in society. AME was created after the African Methodist Episcopal Zion Church. The first churches in Florida were established in Jacksonville, Tallahassee, Quincy, Monticello and Lake City. Black Methodists were treated differently from their White counterparts, including the preachers and bishops. After meeting in homes or beneath brush arbors, they soon built their own churches. In the late 1800s, the Bethel African Methodist Episcopal Church was built in Tallahassee, and the original building served parishioners until 1982.

The early years of growth in the state featured few roads, so spreading the gospel across the area was as big a challenge as taming the wilds of Florida. From town to town, circuit-riding preachers blazed a trail. At first, the waterways were often the most expedient and safest means of travel, although unreliable at times due to weather extremes. They came by rowboat, sailboat, steamboat and riverboat. They traveled on foot, on horseback or by horse and buggy. When rail service and the Model T provided safer and

The horse-and-buggy was soon replaced by the Model T. Separate entrances for men and women were a part of this Madison County church. Photo circa 1900. *Courtesy of the State Archives of Florida.*

faster ways to travel, grand plans were made to build elaborate cathedrals as well as simple meetinghouses. The struggles our pioneer settlers experienced were not overshadowed by the taming of a subtropical wilderness. Searching for spiritual guidance, these pioneers and preachers traveled deep into unexplored and rolling wooded countryside to enhance the frontier culture.

With fertile soil and good climate, early settlers were encouraged to build communities establishing an environment of mutual protection as well as providing for educational and religious needs. The history of a church tells you a lot about the history of an area. With names like Lick Skillet, Two Egg, Tater Hill Bluff and Rattlesnake and the long-forgotten names such as Mosquito County, Mellonville, Cowford, Hogtown, and Alligator, the history of Florida is as colorful as its founders.

Railroads at first had little observable impact on rural communities, but the Chipley line across the Panhandle, the Cross State line from Fernandina to Cedar Key, the St. Augustine to Palm Beach line and the Jacksonville to Key West line did a lot to encourage growth in towns along the routes by making access easier. Tourism and winter visitors promoted the growth of charming hotels and resorts, some of which exist today. Communities wanted houses of worship—if only seasonal, to meet the needs of the influx of tourists, or year-round for their own growing populations. Railroad and cattle barons heard the cry for community churches. Land was donated, and local materials were used to build cathedrals and chapels.

Tithes and talent only go partway toward the completion of a church. Members and ministers have long provided support for church building in the face of limited resources and skills. With the help of the church community through fundraisers and the team efforts of choir directors, Sunday school teachers, deacons, church secretaries and others taking care of the day-to-day responsibilities of the church, the construction of a new building is more than lumber and glass and paint. It is home to the spirit of all those who contributed to its creation.

Some historic churches appear largely unchanged. They sit nestled in their original location as a monument to the town where they were built, appearing much as they did decades ago. Today you might find what was once a rural church along a busy highway. Some have been moved, some remodeled, others extensively modified; some have books written about them. Others are lost, only to be found in old photographs, such as Christ Congregational Church, New Smyrna and an original First Methodist Church in Tampa. Many are listed on the National Register of Historic Places.

A sad-looking old church sits atop a grassy knoll at a fork in the road where an old U.S. highway splits off to make way for a new highway. The grass is overgrown, obscuring the path to the rubble that once served as steps leading to the sanctuary. Another church was repurposed as a home or lodge for guests along a quiet riverside with the remains of a baptismal dock still in the water. A home now fills the sanctuary of one that once opened its doors to small-town worshippers. Another sits empty along the shores of a lake in what was once a frontier town with a promising future. With a reverence for antiquity and a curiosity about the past, you can explore the history of a state and expose events that shaped the area of its ancestors. Unknown towns and rural communities inspire wonder when you question how it all began and why in a specific place.

Hometowns helped create a spirit of heavenly existence on earth, and small towns were the backbone of the state, which provided a fertile growing environment for fields and for families to move forward and explore the larger world. Ecclesiastical structures were often built to inspire awe and wonder in communities as one contemplated the divine and sacred presence of God. Many historic churches have been lost to decay, destruction by hurricanes or war and demolition in the name of progress, only remembered through historic photos.

Some churches now have a secular purpose. They have been transformed into museums or history centers, homes or storage sheds, part of park systems or living heritage sites. Others are crumbling. Many of the buildings were constructed to reflect the majesty of God, and their breathtaking beauty survives. Others were austere and without unnecessary embellishments as a reflection of their founder's belief in focusing on the Christian message, not the building in which it was delivered.

Cathedral, chapel, community church or any place a congregation meets, these houses of worship in Florida go back more than two hundred years. Standing strong, they are treasures to behold for their beauty. A house of worship can be both lovely and simple. The simplicity of the architecture of many small-town and country churches is reflected throughout Florida. In search of a place to reflect and nurture body and soul, pioneers built many treasures of the state seeking not only a haven for worship but also a beautiful space in which to do it. To fully appreciate these creations, it takes a sense of wonder and a slower pace. Searching for relics of Old Florida, traveling along timeworn highways off the beaten path, you might discover a small woodland church and be inspired to follow the footsteps of circuit riders and other ministers of God's word, as they struggled to spread the gospel amid hardships such as heat, hurricanes, tropical storms, disease, mosquitos, wars, fires and financial hardships.

As you look for a lovely crossroads church or island beauty, these handsome little churches with their quiet charm continue to instill awe and wonder. Hearing the quiet crunch of a crushed-shell road, driving along a sandy street or following the ocean breezes and echoing waves beckon you to keep going to discover what lies ahead. Whether walking along a former railroad path, strolling by a sandy beach along the Gulf of Mexico or promenading down a revitalized Main Street, a community church is usually not far away. Whether a multipurpose wood-frame building or a precious Carpenter Gothic jewel, these rare beauties dot both urban and rural communities across the state like coins tossed in a fountain. A church is more than a building. It begins long before the church bells ring, with people seeking salvation and searching for solace in the quiet sanctuary. The beauty in the architectural structure of small churches or elaborate cathedrals creates a magically meaningful place.

This book is intended to serve as a guide to the towns and communities in Florida that are home to these historic landmarks. To see the exteriors of these churches in photographs or in person may help people further

Old church once located in Vernon, Washington County, with Bama, Dorie and Lucy, circa 1910. *Courtesy of the State Archives of Florida.*

appreciate the historical lore and facts left by the pioneers who settled in Florida. Most church congregations began long before a building was conceived, so the building dates are usually later than when the group of worshippers first gathered. Dates listed are as historically accurate as the information found on historic markers provided by the Florida Department of State, the National Register of Historic Places and church websites and in books.

The often-overlooked sacrifices of pioneers help lay the foundation for the little churches scattered across the state as we proceed along mostly paved roads and scenic highways to enjoy their beauty. Enter this journey with a spirit of gratefulness as you soak in the quiet dignity of such holy places. With nostalgia and looking to the future, capturing these churches with photos is a way to show respect for the past and our early pioneers. The spiritual landscape of our country is changing, but not all the church bells have fallen silent. Before they are destroyed by the forces of nature, simply left abandoned or torn down, discover these treasures region by region, from the Spanish Colonial structures of St. Augustine and the Keys with their rich Catholic heritage to the roughhewn timber of simple Florida vernacular, such as Moss Hill Methodist Church in the Panhandle, to the strong English Protestant influence of the richly designed Gothic Revival and Carpenter Gothic styles scattered throughout the state.

Chapter 1

THE SITE OF AMERICA'S FIRST CHURCH

St. Augustine

*Quaint, old, dead-alive Spanish town of the Middle Ages…retains at once
its individuality and its unlikeness to anything else in America* [with] *a
dilapidated old Cathedral with its quaint Moorish belfry, forming one of the
"sights" of St. Augustine.*
—*George M. Barbour,* Florida for Tourists, Invalids, and Settlers, *1882*

Fighting for freedom of religion was a driving force behind the discovery of Florida and a zealous desire to spread Christianity around the world. Greeted by various tribes of Indigenous people, European explorers tromped across the state in search of treasures, while many were on a mission to save the souls of the Indigenous people. Wars of religion between Catholics and Huguenots ensued. When Juan Ponce de León first sighted land on the East Coast, near St. Augustine, in 1513, he named the peninsula Florida and claimed it for Spain. He then sailed on to the Charlotte Harbor area. On returning in 1521, he brought with him colonists and priests in a failed attempt to convert Natives to the Catholic faith. That was the beginning of an epic struggle to spread Christianity across the land.

In 1528, Pánfilo de Narváez landed in Florida near Tampa Bay with Franciscan friars and secular priests to evangelize Native Americans as they moved up the peninsula. A secular or diocesan priest is one who is ordained to serve a diocese; Franciscan friars are known for their devotion, charity, simplicity and sharing of possessions, which others would consider a life of poverty. About a decade later, in 1539, Hernando de Soto arrived near the same area with a small army of soldiers and livestock, along with several priests and friars. As they traveled north, they reached the Tallahassee area, and it is believed they celebrated the first Florida Christmas there. Another Spanish explorer, Tristán de Luna, established a Catholic colony on Pensacola Bay in 1559 with soldiers, colonists and Dominican friars. A storm destroyed their ships and what little provisions they had. After struggling to survive in a new land for over a year, this attempt at establishing Florida's first permanent settlement failed.

In 1562, an attempt at a permanent claim in Florida came from the protestant French Huguenots, who were seeking freedom from the religious persecution they faced in their homeland. Later, in 1568, that first Protestant colony established in Florida was destroyed by an army of Spaniards from St. Augustine. But under the leadership of Jean Ribault, with René de Laudonnière, these Frenchmen successfully landed on the shores of northeast Florida near the mouth of what today is known as the St. Johns River. On arrival, Ribault and company knelt in prayer and gave thanks for their safe arrival, making this possibly the first Protestant prayer by an organized religion in Florida. The next day, after selecting a spot where it might be easily seen entering the port, along the south side of the river, Ribault and his men erected a stone column with the French king's coat of arms carved into it, thereby claiming the area for France. René de Laudonnière returned to the area two years later, in 1564, to build what would be Fort Caroline (later named San Mateo). He was welcomed by a group of local Native Americans, who led them to the stone column left by Ribault. It was adorned with flowers and fruit. Artist Jacques le Moyne traveled with Laudonnière and captured the event in one of his many drawings. In 1591, Theodor de Bry published a book of the drawings with commentary. The following description is from *Discovering the New World, Based on the Works of Theodore de Bry*, edited by Michael Alexander.

> *During the second voyage in Florida under Laudonnière's command, that leader went ashore with twenty-five arquebusiers. He was greeted by the Indians who had gathered in crowds to see the new arrivals. Their king, Athore, who lived five or six miles inland from there, welcomed them with great kindness and presented Laudonnière with gifts. He then gave the French to understand that he wished to show them something remarkable and begged them to follow him. They agreed, but seeing how many natives surrounded them, proceeded with caution. He conducted them to the island where Ribault had erected on a hillock the stone column engraved with the*

arms of the king of France. On approaching the French saw the Indians worshipping the stone as an idol. The chief, having saluted it with the respect that his subjects were used to accord him, kissed it and the other Indians did likewise. Afterwards the French were encouraged to do the same. Before the monument lay baskets filled with the country's fruit, vases full of perfumed oils, roots both edible and medicinal, and a bow and arrows. From top to bottom the stone was wreathed with flowers of all kinds and branches of the rarest trees. After watching the rituals of these wretched barbarians, the French rejoined their companions in looking for the most suitable place to build a small fort. The king, Athore, is a handsome man, wise, honourable and strong, more than half a foot taller than even the tallest of our men. His modest gravity lends majesty to his already noble bearing. He married his mother and had by her several children of both sexes whom he proudly introduced to us, striking his thigh as he did so. It might be added that after he married his mother his father, Satourioua, ceased to live with her.

The first Anglican service was possibly held in 1565 onboard an English naval ship while anchored in the St. Johns River, waiting to come ashore at Fort Caroline. It would be two centuries later before English Anglicans worshipped on land during the Florida British Period from 1763 to 1783.

1565–1763: First Spanish Period

In August 1565, Pedro Menéndez of Spain sighted Florida on the Catholic-designated feast day of Saint Augustine. Menéndez came with a missionary and a military zeal to teach and convert Native Americans to the Catholic faith while teaching them to read and write. Franciscans later learned the Timucua language to better communicate their religious convictions to the tribes. Menéndez continued sailing around the area searching for a place to establish a permanent settlement on the land he considered belonging to Spain. This included a geographical area with far more territory than the present peninsula.

Menéndez named the town St. Augustine and proclaimed it "Nombre de Dios" (in the Name of God). It was here that Spanish pioneers founded the first mission in the United States for North American Indians. In the Catholic faith, a mission is considered a non-self-supporting congregation, as opposed to a parish, which is a self-supporting congregation.

Father Francisco López de Mendoza Grajales, a Spanish diocesan priest, created an altar, and when Menéndez came ashore, Father López held a high cross and celebrated the nation's first parish Mass at the landing spot. Today the historic marker in the area reads: "On this site, September 8, 1565, Pedro Menéndez de Aviles landed with a band of settlers to found St. Augustine and established the first permanent Christian settlement in the United States."

Father Francisco Pareja of Spain compiled grammar and devotional books in the Timucuan language, the first known work compiled in any Native American language. Therefore, the Spanish had the trust and help of local tribes when they massacred the French in an attack following Mass. Menéndez captured Fort Caroline in 1565 and renamed it San Mateo; the Spanish were then in full control of the area as they ushered in the mission era of Florida's history.

In 1586, the British were interested in this new land, beginning another religious battle. Sir Francis Drake and his troops landed at the public square, where they sacked and burned down most of the city, including the original parish church, before returning to England. Later Spanish colonists built the chapel of Nuestra Señora de la Soledad (Our Lady of Solitude) on St. George Street south of today's Cathedral Basilica. The historic marker at the site states it was built after 1572. The hospital that was attached in 1597 became the first one in the continental United States. Destroyed by fire in 1599 and again in 1605, the chapel was enlarged into a church in 1687. In the 1600s, at the site of Mission Nombre de Dios, Spanish colonists also built the Chapel of Our Lady of La Leche to honor Nuestra Señora de la Leche (Our Lady of La Leche, or the Nursing Madonna). The National Shrine of Our Lady of La Leche is a sacred place and the oldest shrine in the United States. Destroyed in 1728 during a British siege, it was rebuilt by 1875 and restored in 1914 after hurricane damage. The area features an 11-foot bronze statue of Father López to honor his role in the birth of Christianity, and in 1965, a 208-foot stainless steel cross was also erected there to mark where the cross of Christianity was first placed. When it came time to do battle against the French, both the French Huguenots and the Spanish Catholics sought spiritual guidance as they fought in the name of God.

As religion grew stronger, so did places of worship. Nuestra Señora de la Soledad and other buildings in the area were built or rebuilt beginning about 1736, using solid coquina stone. Coquina stone is found and quarried along the northeast coast of Florida, and Anastasia Island provided an almost

Entrance to the Catholic Chapel at Castillo de San Marcos, a.k.a. Fort Marion, St. Augustine, St. Johns County, circa 1900. *Courtesy of the State Archives of Florida.*

endless supply for constructing fireproof churches and forts. The unique composition of this stone is the result of thousands of years of crushed coquina shells and other sea life being pounded by waves along the shore to create a solid mass that was exposed to the elements when sea levels began to drop. The blocks of cut stone for Nuestra Señora de la Soledad were quarried from Anastasia Island, and the people of St. Augustine worshipped there until 1763. All the while, from 1672 until 1695, the Spanish were building Castillo de San Marcos of coquina stone to replace nine successive wooden fortifications—which also served as a safe place to worship during battle. The Catholic chapel, with altar and holy water, located inside the fort along the north side gives an idea of how important religion was to Spanish soldiers and citizens, providing them a place of worship when the town was under attack. In 1825, the name was changed to Fort Marion, then changed back to Castillo de San Marcos in 1942 after it became a National Monument and Park and open for tours. The chapel was described in the booklet *St. Augustine Under Three Flags: Tourist Guide and History*:

> *At the north side of the court, directly opposite the sallyport, is the chapel. The entrance to this room was very ornamental. This work, which had become nearly obliterated by the action of the elements, has recently been*

reconstructed by the War Department, great care being taken in following the original plans, which were obtained from the Spanish Government. Entering, we see on each side the niches for holy water; just beyond, on the right, pieces of cedar imbedded in the masonry mark the place where the confessional was fastened to the wall. At the rear is a raised stone platform for the altar, and above the altar a large niche where stood the patron saint, Saint Augustine. Looking up, we see near the spring of the arch the ends of the old timbers which supported the platform for the choir. Directly overhead, near the middle of the room, is a square hole from which hung an immense wooden cross called the rood. On either side of the chapel are doorways through the iron bars of which the prisoners could hear mass before being executed. The bars were necessary, as if a prisoner gained access to a chapel and knelt at the altar, he could claim the right of sanctuary.

When Spain ceded Florida to the British in 1763, Nuestra Señora de la Soledad was converted into St. Peter's Anglican Church, and a wooden spire, a clock and a bell tower facing west were added; the former Spanish entrance faced east. The parish church area was used as parade grounds for the troops, and the Franciscan monastery located there became a barracks.

1763–1783: British Period

The Spanish missions of the 1600s that were multiplying across North Florida, from St. Augustine to Tallahassee, came to an end when the British took control of the state in 1763. As a part of the Treaty of Paris, Spain gave Florida to England in exchange for Cuba. Land grants were offered to encourage settlement, so English plantations and homesteads were established. All British colonies were mission fields for the Church of England, and the Florida Spanish missions soon disappeared. The Episcopal influence was felt across North Florida from St. Augustine to Pensacola.

By 1777, Casa Avero, built in 1749 and located about one hundred yards from the city gates of St Augustine, served as a religious center and place of worship for survivors of Dr. Andrew Turnbull's failed New Smyrna colony. Turnbull, a British colonizer, brought over one thousand indentured laborers from the Mediterranean, including the Island of Minorca, to work his indigo plantation. The six hundred survivors, the majority being Minorcans with some Greeks and Italians as well, walked seventy miles to Saint Augustine, where many settled on Charlotte Street to start a new life. Today, the Saint Photios Greek Orthodox National Shrine and Museum on George Street describes their journey.

1783–1821: SECOND SPANISH PERIOD

After twenty years of British rule and the end of the American Revolution, Florida was returned to Spain as part of the second Treaty of Paris, which ended the war in 1783. St. Augustine became the religious center of Spanish Florida, while St. Peter's Anglican Church went into decay. Lack of Spanish oversight led to conflicts and provoked the Seminole Wars. The Catholic church was revived, but it was eventually dismantled, and the stone was possibly used in the building of a new parish church, the current Cathedral Basilica on the plaza, to replace the old parish church on St. George Street. In 1793, the Cathedral of St. Augustine cornerstone was laid, and the Roman Catholic church was completed in 1797. Bells were hung in the niches across the top portion of the façade. They were rung by hand with wooden mallets from a wooden platform until the fire of 1887 destroyed the platform and most of the church. Only the façade and a portion of the exterior walls of the church survived the fire, which destroyed the roof and interior. At the time, Henry Flagler was building the Ponce de Leon Hotel and witnessed the fire along with architect James Renwick, who designed New York's St. Patrick's Cathedral and the Smithsonian Castle. Both men offered their services in reconstructing the church. The original church was without a tower or steeple, and Flagler contributed a six-story bell tower. Renwick offered to help with the design and enlargement. During restoration, the church was extended twelve feet beyond the original north wall and a freestanding bell tower was added. The transepts, bell tower and extended nave were added in poured concrete rather than the old coquina. This beautiful Cathedral Basilica with eighteenth-century Spanish architecture and a nineteenth-century bell tower still stands today as a monument to the dedication and perseverance of our forefathers. It has been restored to look much like it did in the late 1700s. (In 1870, it was upgraded to a cathedral. For its historical, spiritual and architectural significance, it was raised to the status of a minor basilica by Pope Paul VI in 1976.)

The mission-style façade of the Cathedral of St. Augustine reflects the Spanish influence of the era and resembles the façade of Nuestra Senora de La Leche. Photo circa 1871. *Courtesy of the State Archives of Florida.*

Cathedral of St. Augustine, circa 1900. *Courtesy of the State Archives of Florida.*

Father Miguel O'Reilly, an Irish priest, supervised the completion of construction and formally opened the 1797 church. He served as a chaplain to the Spanish troops and bought a house at 32 Aviles Street, which served as the parish rectory in 1785. Since 1866, the rectory has been occupied by the Sisters of St. Joseph and is now a house museum and archival repository.

1821–1845: TERRITORIAL PERIOD

In 1821, the United States took possession of Florida from Spain, and it became a U.S. territory. At that time, the only known Protestant church in Florida was Pigeon Creek Baptist Church in Nassau County. That church is remembered with a granite marker describing it as the oldest Baptist church in Florida, organized in 1821. Early meetings were held under a brush arbor, which was followed by two log houses of worship. The church on that location today was built in 1956. In 1823, John Slade was among the first preachers to bring the gospel to the Territory of Florida, and for that he is often called the Father of Methodism in Florida. Slate also wrote: "We may safely say that the first Protestant preaching in Florida was on Amelia Island," which contradicts the claim of the Pigeon Creek Baptist Church. In the 1800s, records were scarce, and information traveled slowly, but today we can put the pieces together to come up with more details of the birth of religious denominations in Florida. To support local congregations, the Florida Baptist State Convention was organized in 1854 in the home of Baptist minister Richard J. Mays in Madison.

Chapter 2

NEW TOWNS, NEW TERRITORY, NEW STATE

[St. Augustine society was] *heterogeneous, transitory, and collected from all parts of the world, some with polished intellect and more with neither intellect nor polish.*
—*Joseph L. Smith, a vestryman of Trinity Church, 1825*

The British period in Florida was sandwiched between two Spanish periods, and the opportunity for growth of the Church of England (also known as the Anglican Church) faltered until the territorial period had begun. St. Peter's Anglican Church was returned to the Spanish in ruins, but once again, it was a place for Catholics to worship. Then Spain ceded the distant and wild territory of Florida to the United States in 1821. Although many Spanish Catholics left, enough stayed, and the small Catholic church eventually was designated Cathedral Basilica of St. Augustine. A cathedral in the Catholic church is run by a bishop and is the main church of the diocese.

Territorial Florida saw rapid growth as new settlers migrated from the Carolinas through Georgia to the unexplored wilderness of piney woods and sand hills in North Florida. East and West Florida became one and Tallahassee the capital city. Around that time, Baptist, Methodist, Presbyterian and Episcopal services were held, meeting in courthouses, homes and barns or under brush arbors. The Baptists mostly organized in rural areas, and the Methodists enjoyed the services of circuit-riding preachers throughout North Florida. The Presbyterians were few, but they continued to grow in number.

The Protestant Episcopal Church in St. Augustine held its first services in the Government House. By 1825, a cornerstone had been laid for a new church, and the Trinity Parish Episcopal Church faced the plaza opposite the Cathedral Basilica. It was completed in 1831, making it the oldest Protestant church building in Florida and the first in the Gothic Revival style. The Gothic Revival style established an architectural design that helped convey the function of the building and played an important role in the construction of some of the most charming churches built in towns and rural areas throughout Florida. The Episcopal Church is an American offshoot of the Anglican Church, or Church of England, and is centered in the United States, while the Anglican church is based in the United Kingdom.

As churches were built in Florida, commonalities within each Christian church denomination could be seen. The Episcopal churches tended to be more elaborate, while the Methodist churches were often unembellished, simple square or rectangular buildings. The Baptist structures were even more basic and often left unpainted.

In 1831, the entrance of Trinity Parish Episcopal Church faced the plaza. When the church was expanded to the west in 1903, the entrance was reoriented to face St. George Street. The original 1831 part of Trinity Parish Episcopal Church was preserved as the north transept and is now the

Trinity Parish Episcopal Church, St. Augustine, St. Johns County, circa 1909. *Courtesy of the State Archives of Florida.*

Chapel of St. Peter. In a cross-shaped church, the nave is the central part of the building where the congregation sits, or the main body of the building; the transept is the area forming the arms at right angles from the nave. On June 5, 1834, Bishop Nathaniel Bowen formally consecrated the church. The spire was added around 1843. The chapel features many stained-glass windows, including a triptych above the altar and a rare, signed Louis Comfort Tiffany window, added in 1905. The triptych window was funded by a group of young girls who raised money to purchase and dedicate it to Bishop Bowen to honor his years of service and devotion from 1874 to 1884.

By 1838, seven Episcopal parishes were organized to form a diocese, and six of the churches are still in use today. The seal of the diocese today features seven golden stars representing the seven original churches. Trinity Parish Episcopal in St. Augustine, as mentioned above, was the first. The members of the former St. Joseph Episcopal Church in the Panhandle, now St. James Episcopal Church, no longer worship in the original building, but the new St. James Episcopal Church received its charter from the Territory of Florida in 1835. It was refounded in 1931 and became a parish in 1962.

The other five churches are Christ Church, Pensacola; St. John's Episcopal Church, Tallahassee; St. Paul's Episcopal Church, Key West; Christ Church (now Trinity Episcopal Church), Apalachicola; and St. John's Episcopal Church (now St. John's Cathedral), Jacksonville. The following is a brief description of the five churches.

Today, Old Christ Church Pensacola on Seville Square in Historic Pensacola Village is a part of living history programs and no longer used as a church. Services were once held there from 1832 to 1903, and during the Civil War, Union Federal soldiers used the church as a barracks and later as a military chapel. In 1865, it was once again a church, and it was remodeled in 1879. A new Christ Church, Pensacola, was built downtown, and the old stained-glass windows were transferred there in 1902. From 1903 until 1905, the St. Cyprians congregations used the old church building, but then it was left abandoned until the early 1930s. In 1936, the City of Pensacola acquired the title to use the building as a library and later as the Pensacola Historical Museum, which it is now.

When St. John's Episcopal Church, Tallahassee, was established in 1827, services were held in the courthouse. In 1838, the first church was constructed in a classical style out of wood with a portico and four pillars. It was one of the few churches not seriously damaged during the Civil War, but the marble marker at the newer church on North Monroe Street indicates it was destroyed by fire in 1879 and rebuilt in 1880. Bishop John Freeman Young laid the

Christ Church, a.k.a. Old Christ Church, Pensacola, Escambia County, circa 1897. *Courtesy of the State Archives of Florida.*

cornerstone for a new one-story red brick Gothic Revival church building, and in 1881, the first services were held while the church was still under construction. After storm damage and delays in building, it was consecrated in 1888. An old brick retaining wall and large square bell tower add to the historic beauty of the church.

When it was completed in 1841, St. Paul's Episcopal Church was the only place of worship in Key West, according to Episcopal Church historian Edgar Legare Pennington. It was built with 450 pieces of native coral rock. The church was rebuilt after a hurricane in 1846 and destroyed by fire in 1886; the third church was completed in 1887. Another hurricane damaged the church in the early 1900s, and it was rebuilt in 1919 in the Gothic Revival style as it stands today, using native coral stone. The stained-glass windows were installed over eighty years, starting around 1920.

The Florida man with the creative mind behind air-conditioning, John Gorrie, helped found Apalachicola's first church, Christ Church, Apalachicola, which became Trinity Episcopal Church. This Greek Revival frame structure with Ionic columns and a bell tower was completed between

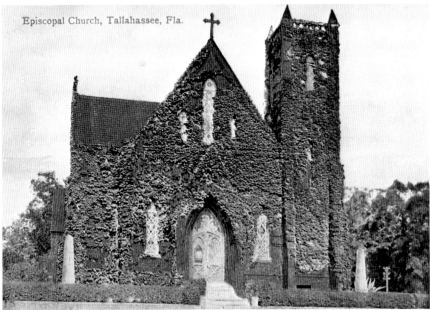

This page: The first St. John's Episcopal Church, *top*, (photo circa 1830) and the new church on Monroe Street, *bottom*, (photo circa 1900), Tallahassee, Leon County. *Courtesy of the State Archives of Florida.*

Opposite: St. Paul's Episcopal Church, Key West, Monroe County. *Author's collection.*

1838 and 1841 using prefabricated parts made in upstate New York and sent to Apalachicola by ship. It was reassembled with peg fasteners instead of nails.

Sitting atop Billy Goat Hill, the highest point in Jacksonville, the current St. John's Cathedral was built after fire destroyed the previous churches on the same site. A small wooden chapel was built while plans were being made for a Gothic Revival cathedral, which was rebuilt on the original

Trinity Episcopal Church, a.k.a Christ Church, Apalachicola, Franklin County, circa 1884. *Courtesy of the State Archives of Florida.*

foundation. Construction began in 1902 after the Great Fire of 1901, and the church was completed in 1906. The new church features stained-glass windows and a bell tower.

The first three Episcopal bishops of Florida can be credited with bringing some of the most beautiful ecclesiastical architectural designs to the state. From 1851 until 1866, Francis Huger Rutledge served as the first bishop of Florida. Before that, he was rector of Trinity Parish Episcopal Church in St. Augustine, then of St. John's, Tallahassee, for seven years. John Freeman Young became the second bishop of Florida from 1867 until 1885. An 1845 graduate of Virginia Theological Seminary in Alexandria, not only did he pioneer the growth of Episcopal parishes in Florida, but he also translated the German Christmas carol "Stille Nacht! Heilige Nacht!" into the English version, "Silent Night," while serving as an assistant minister at Trinity Church in New York. There he met English-born architect Richard Upjohn, known as the Father of American Gothic Architecture. Upjohn's architectural designs revived Gothic architecture in the United States and created a new, more affordable style termed Carpenter Gothic. What was once built of stone could now be created with the same grace from wood, and a high level of craftsmanship could be achieved using local talent and timber. Under Upjohn's influence, Young developed a deep appreciation for Upjohn's architectural style and is responsible for the beautiful design of many Episcopal churches found throughout Florida.

The Civil War left the state disorganized and impoverished, and it required great sacrifices to build churches. Young was attracted to Florida by the pioneer work of the first settlers in making a home for themselves in this new territory. He was very active in mission building for the Episcopal Church, and Carpenter Gothic became a standard architectural style for small Episcopal congregations in early Florida settlements. Young traveled as many circuit riders did—on horseback, in buggies and carts, by steamer and sailboat and sometimes on foot—to start missions and build or rebuild churches. He helped select the sites for Episcopal churches and promoted the use of Upjohn's Carpenter Gothic–style architecture in pioneer Florida settlements. Historian Pennington praised his foresight in the selection of church sites. At Cocoa Beach, Young went into a wooded area by the river with an ax and started preparing the site for the Episcopal church, which still stands today, although altered to accommodate the growing congregation.

Traveling from Jacksonville to Key West, Bishop Young reported in 1880 that eleven churches had been built or were in the process of being built. He visited Cedar Key and Tampa before traveling south to Key West. Young noted in his journal of 1883 that the physical as well as spiritual well-being of all creatures is important, explaining why building a church in a community is meaningful and enduring. Young also organized the first Episcopal church exclusively for Blacks and a Spanish-language parish for Cuban immigrants, both in Key West. In a tribute to Young, Bishop Edwin Gardner Weed, the third bishop of Florida, noted that not only was he a master builder, but his foresight in the selection of places to build churches was also remarkable.

Weed was the Episcopal bishop of Florida from 1886 until 1892. Whereas Young went from isolated settlement to isolated settlement by steamer or twelve-hour horse-and-buggy ride, Bishop Weed traveled by railroad to remote areas. When Bishop Weed died in 1924, he had spent thirty-eight of his seventy-seven years as the bishop of Florida. When the diocese split, Bishop William Crane Gray oversaw the South Florida District, and more churches were constructed in the southern part of the state. Young and Weed both promoted Carpenter Gothic designs developed by Upjohn.

Upjohn incorporated many aspects of Late Gothic Revival features into his plans for an economical yet still attractive wooden church design. Using local craftsmen and lumber were also important to reduce the cost of building

St. Mark's Episcopal Church, Palatka, Putnam County, circa 1854. *Courtesy of the State Archives of Florida.*

in rural areas. St. Mark's Episcopal Church, the oldest Upjohn-inspired design along the St. Johns River, can still be found in Palatka. In general, this style was able to satisfy financial restrictions with simple board-and-batten wood-frame buildings. St. Mark's served as a Civil War meeting place and barracks for Federal troops. By the close of the war, it had deteriorated, with a rotting belfry. Reopened in 1866, it was enlarged and altered many times. The rose window over the main entrance is still intact. A very tall bell tower was later added and holds an Episcopal cross atop the spire.

Before railroads and roadways were established, settlers were isolated, with no reliable system of communication. Travel was difficult for frontier ministers as well as early pioneers. The wilderness was home to these newcomers as well as bears, panthers and wildcats in the forests, while alligators and water moccasins were at home in the swamps. Yet these pioneers found one another and created a haven from the wearies of the world. Missionaries came by boat, bicycle, on foot and on horseback carrying clothing, books and the Holy Bible. Ministers traveled from one community to another and church to church, at times filling in for other denominations. They went on to set up schools and other educational institutions.

According to *Religion on Florida's Territorial Frontier*, by Ernest F. Dibble, Florida was about to enter a new era, with hotels, boardinghouses, churches and universities on the horizon. "The first American Universities were founded for the instruction of clergy," and this is reflected in the history of both Florida State University and the University of Florida. According to the State Archives of Florida,

> *Before the University of Florida was founded by legislative act in 1905, with Gainesville as its location, the city was served and was proud to be served by, the East Florida Seminary. The community was proud enough of the Seminary that when it burned in 1883, public funds were subscribed and a $12,000 debt taken on to rebuild.... The academic building now is part of the Methodist Church, at 419 Northeast 1st street in Gainesville, and is called Epworth Hall. Epworth Hall was later added to the National Register of Historic Places in 1973. The girl's [sic] dormitory became the White House hotel after the Seminary was discontinued when the University of Florida was founded; as a hotel, it served the city many years, until it burned. East Florida Seminary was the name given to a school founded in 1853 by the Methodist Church. The school was troubled financially and was suspended after the Civil War. An existing state school in Ocala took up the name, and later was moved to Gainesville and merged with the Gainesville Academy, which itself*

was founded in the 1850s. East Florida Seminary, when organized by the state legislature, was maintained to serve the 22 Florida counties east of the Suwannee River; its counterpart, West Florida Seminary in Tallahassee, was to serve Middle and West Florida. Both of the seminaries had their original beginnings in territorial days, when Congress donated townships of land for the support of such institutions.

By the time Florida was granted statehood in 1845, the growth of churches was beginning to take off. While primitive churches and traditional meetinghouses were still being constructed in rural Florida, more decorative Carpenter Gothic churches and elaborate cathedrals were coming to life. The painted meetinghouse or the old country church with its unpainted clapboard served its purpose just as the decorative ones did. The late 1850s was a time of population growth with new communities and the division of larger counties. Many were destroyed, but some pre–Civil War churches still stand today.

St. Luke's Episcopal Church, Marianna, Jackson County, circa 1900. There have been four buildings on this site. This photo shows the third building, constructed in 1879, destroyed by fire in 1941. *Courtesy of the State Archives of Florida.*

Moss Hill Methodist Church, Vernon, Washington County. *Courtesy of Pat and Carolyn Sheffield.*

St. Luke's Episcopal Church, Marianna, was founded in 1838, and its first building was constructed in a modified Gothic style in 1854. It was rebuilt in 1862, but St. Luke's was in the middle of a Marianna Civil War skirmish in 1864. Union troops burned the church down. One Union officer saved the church Bible and gave it to the rector. A third church was built in 1879, but it fell victim to an accidental fire in 1941. The bell was the only thing saved. The present Gothic-style building was completed in 1947.

Bethel United Methodist Church, a.k.a. Old Bethel Church, was organized in the town of Alligator, and the simple church building standing today was constructed in 1855. In 1859, the name of the town was changed to the more inviting Lake City in Columbia County. For over a century, it has been known to locals as "the white church by the side of the road."

Many beautiful Florida place names are only simple descriptors of an area, and Moss Hill is a community with such a name, home to Moss Hill Methodist Church. The unpainted wood frame that has weathered to a silver-gray was built during the territorial days of Florida. A stagecoach route ran near the property. Made of a rough-hewn heart pine, the horizontal siding and gable roof are supported by a brick pier foundation. Frontier

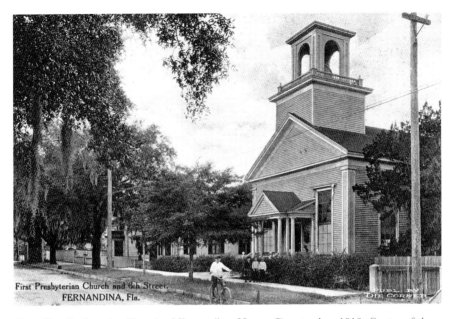

First Presbyterian Church and 6th Street.
FERNANDINA, Fla.

Above: First Presbyterian Church of Fernandina, Nassau County, circa 1910. *Courtesy of the State Archives of Florida.*

Opposite: Old Philadelphia Presbyterian Church, Quincy, Gadsden County, circa 1959. *Courtesy of the State Archives of Florida.*

construction was simple and durable. Once it's saturated with sap and aged, the heart pine becomes strong and impervious to termites or water damage. The two doors were designed to have one entrance for women and girls and one for men and boys. According to information found on the Altha Methodist Church historical marker in Calhoun County, the Moss Hill Methodist Church was built by Daniel Thomas Richards in 1857.

The history of the town once simply called Fernandina, now Fernandina Beach, predates the Civil War. The First Presbyterian Church of Fernandina is in a quiet island neighborhood. In 1858, this simple frame church was built on land donated by David L. Yulee, a Jewish immigrant and Florida's first U.S. senator. Federal troops occupied the building during the Civil War, and a Union officer saved the bell from being melted for armament. That original bell is still in use today. According to Suzanne Davis Hardee in *The Golden Age of Amelia Island, The Churches*, an entrance porch was added around the beginning of the twentieth century.

Old Philadelphia Presbyterian Church in Quincy, Gadsden County, was built in 1859 as a simple frame clapboard church to replace an 1828 log

meetinghouse. Services were held at the church until 1912. The historic marker at the sight reads in part:

> Presbyterians came to this area from Georgia and the Carolinas as early as 1822. These worshippers built Philadelphia, a log meeting house, in 1828. This log structure was replaced in 1859 by the present building. Philadelphia served until 1912 as a house of worship, a place of education, and a center of community life. Many Presbyterian churches in Florida and southern Georgia trace their origins to Philadelphia.

Old Philadelphia Presbyterian Church was served by itinerant ministers until 1832. This was a common practice among newly formed churches in frontier territory. The spread of religion continued across North Florida from St. Augustine to Pensacola and south to Gainesville and on to Key West.

Chapter 3

CIRCUIT-RIDING PREACHERS
AND OTHER MEN OF GOD

Wherever men can go for money, we can go for the love of Christ and for souls.
—Motto of Methodist circuit rider John Cole Ley

Seminole Indians and Crackers, plantation owners and slaves were scattered throughout the state. Lighthouses began to warn and welcome those at sea, while forts protected the inland settlers. Post offices and ferry crossings popped up, and steamboats began to ply the rivers, bringing new settlers, invalids and tourists. While most of the forts are long forgotten, many of the lighthouses remain as reminders of the perseverance of those early men and women who crafted plans to build communities that would embrace the freedoms and lifestyles they so desperately sought. At the forefront of bringing religion to and through this untamed territory were circuit-riding ministers. Methodist minister John Cole Ley said, "The apostles were itinerant preachers, and their method of rotating among the churches is the spirit of Methodism today."

The Catholics and Episcopals laid the groundwork for church building in Florida, and the growth continued as the state was established. Pigeon Creek Baptist Church near Callahan in Nassau County was among the first known Protestant churches within the newly established 1821 territory. By 1835, there were eight Baptist churches in Florida. Catholic and Episcopal bishops along with Methodist ministers, Baptist preachers and Presbyterian pastors crisscrossed the state to spread the gospel of Jesus Christ and to bring the comfort of religion to those lonely and isolated communities. Methodism was most likely introduced through circuit riders about 1823. They were soon followed by Baptist, Presbyterian and Episcopal clergy as they helped build churchgoing communities.

From Saddlebags to Satellites, edited by William E. Brooks, shares how the Methodist movement started in Florida, from the first Methodist circuit riders in 1823, when the state was open to Protestantism, to the establishment of churches in the Florida wilderness. Settlers were scattered, but the circuit riders traveled from house to house and settlement to settlement, preaching in homes, in schools or out of doors.

Born in 1790 in South Carolina, John Slade is considered the Father of Methodism in Florida. In 1821, he earned his license to exhort. A Methodist exhorter was a lay speaker given permission to hold meetings, lead prayers and evangelize before becoming an ordained preacher. Enduring the hardships of a circuit rider—such as hunger, thirst, cold and exposure, as well as "insults from unbelievers"—he also found much joy. Slade died in 1854 but left a trail for others to follow.

It was a hard life for circuit riders. They were frequently in the saddle, on a wagon or on foot, following the settlers down dusty dirt roads and across rivers and streams to preach the gospel in the wilderness. They traveled from place to place for weeks at a time, meeting the needs of the few or the many congregants along their circuit. They worked together, supporting one another, and often shared spaces or filled in when one could not make the journey. On the frontier and in the city, they gathered in homes, barns, stables, tents and pine-wood clearings or under moss-covered brush arbors for shade from the Florida sun. The circuit-riding preacher helped encourage settlement in the Florida frontier as the Baptists and Methodists connected isolated communities by bringing news of the many new settlements, along with spiritual comfort. Ley describes in his book, *Fifty-Two Years in Florida*, what it was like for the circuit rider:

> *The traveler of to-day can form but little conception of what it was then. The country was but thinly settled, often there were stretches of forty miles between houses. The roads, especially in the southern part of the district, were chiefly such as had been opened by the troops during the Indian war. The rapid growth of vegetation rendered the roads obscure, and often, for miles, the traveler did not know whether he was on the right road or not; indeed, he was often perplexed to find out if he was on any road....And if he could keep out of too deep water, he would get somewhere sometime, and...wherever he reached a human habitation a cordial welcome awaited*

him, and…when he reached the place for preaching he would meet an eager congregation, some of whom had come many miles to hear the word.

Ley continues his description:

As to roads, at that day we had the King's Highway, from St. Augustine to St. Mary's River, via Cowford (now Jacksonville); the Bellamy road, from Tallahassee to St. Augustine; the Government road, from the Georgia line to Tampa Bay; and a few shorter ones cut by the troops during the war. As to bridges, none. As to ferries, we had some two or three upon the St. John's, and three upon the Suwannee. The small rivers, and creeks we swam. Sometimes a settler would have a dugout [canoe] *and carry the missionary over, while his horse would swim by its side; but generally, he would be alone, and his horse was his only canoe…and sleep in his wet clothes at night.*

As better roads and modes of transportation fostered more settlement, permanent church buildings followed to meet the needs of ever-growing congregations with local ministers. Catholic, Episcopal, Methodist and Baptist men of God traveled throughout the territory that became a state, and many wrote down what they saw and told stories about the towns and people, giving a glimpse into the hardships and joys they encountered. Clergy were welcomed by most without regard to denomination; Florida pioneers desperately wanted to continue to hear God's word to combat the feeling of loneliness in the wilderness.

In the 1820s, the federal government authorized the construction of a road following, in part, an old Native American foot trail and the Old Mission Trail that went from St. Augustine to Pensacola. The section from the territorial capital in Tallahassee to St. Augustine was built by private contractor John Bellamy. The Bellamy Road was completed in 1826. One critic predicted that it would not last a year, with mud and tree stumps making it a bumpy ride, but he was wrong. Sections of the old sand road remain in use today, though it is indeed a bumpy ride. Bellamy Road was vital to the success of mission work and key to spreading religion and church building across North Florida, as it also gave access to areas south in the Florida wilderness.

These men of God were incredibly dedicated. They rode hundreds of miles through swollen swamps and raging waters, crossing creeks and riding through dense backwoods forests with jungle-like vegetation and tangled

Reverend Dwight F. Cameron Jr., a circuit-riding minister in Volusia County, circa 1916.
Courtesy of the State Archives of Florida.

vines. Their limited supplies might include saddlebags with Bible and blanket, clothing and maybe a hymnal, along with food rations for themselves and their horses. Facing danger and disease, they rode through pelting rain and approaching hurricanes with high winds and storm surges. The wintertime cold with near-freezing temperatures was followed by the blazing tropical sun of summer—all while dealing with critters in the wild, such as alligators, panthers, wild boars and bears, along with rattlesnakes. Hunger and thirst were common while circuit riders were exposed to the harsh elements of subtropical Florida.

Many self-supporting ministers were there to meet the spiritual, social and community needs of settlers who came from miles around to hear the word of God. With meager pay and hard work, these preachers covered the rural circuit to hold revivals and organize churches. Many areas were too poor to support a full-time pastor but welcomed these circuit riders into their homes to share what little they had. Early pioneers were looking for comfort, hope, joy and the possibility of establishing a church.

The Catholics were not forsaken in St. Augustine, as the retired Reverend Michael Portier documented during his ventures across the northern part of the state, sharing his experiences in the book *From Pensacola to St. Augustine in 1827: A Journey of the Rt. Rev. Michael Portier*. Born in France in 1795, he came to the United States in 1817 and became the first vicar apostolic of the parishes of Mobile, Pensacola and St. Augustine. Bishop Portier tells his story with touches of humor as he describes his trek from the former capital of western Florida, Pensacola, through Tallahassee, where he celebrated Mass with both Catholics and Protestants, then on to St. Augustine. He felt compelled to visit St. Augustine because of the historical significance of the Catholic Church there, "where the number of faithful was greater than at Pensacola, by the remembrance of the cross that was planted in that part of Florida soon after the discovery of the New World…neglected by its pastors and robbed by mercenaries, was then without spiritual aid.…I burned to cross the wilderness and go to my people." A poetic writer, Portier describes the characters he encountered as he made his way across the northern part of the state, along with the heat, the loneliness and fear, given "the recent outrages perpetrated by a band of Seminole Indians," yet he took solace remembering the promise of Jesus Christ in Luke 21:18: "Not a hair on our head should fall without His consent."

Portier left Pensacola in June 1827, and on the twelfth day of his journey, he reached Tallahassee and celebrated Mass there in a room filled with Protestants. A yellow fever outbreak in St. Augustine kept him in town for weeks, and Portier did not arrive back in Pensacola until October 12. Years before the wilds of the Florida Panhandle were settled, Portier walked and rode his horse following the chain of hills from Pensacola to Tallahassee to St. Augustine. The difficulties of traversing the state before ferries, freeways, bridges and boardinghouses is reflected in comments such as, "Nothing so tends to make a man feel his helplessness and his need of companionship as those lonely journeys through new and unfrequented territory." On one occasion, he dined on bear steak, watermelon and tasty terrapin soup, yet after days of travel and little nourishment, he welcomed the stale bacon and hot cornbread offered to him for breakfast. The natural beauty of the virgin lands he witnessed—the forests of pines, magnolia, laurel, cedar and cypress trees—was tinged with the annoyance of horseflies, gnats and mosquitoes. He discovered waterfalls, streams and springs with caverns and caves along the way, but he refrained from trying to bathe. It wasn't worth the risk of not only alligators but also rattlesnakes and moccasins.

Traveling with a farmer and a mail carrier, Portier noted, "Believing in the divinity was a common bond regardless of religious denomination." Inspired by the Bible verse "I can do all things in Him which strengthened me" (Phil. 4:13), he continued his journey. Travel companions changed, and they stayed in the homes of strangers along the way. At times, he was forced to sleep outside in the woods and swampy areas, crossing rivers with or without the help of ferry services. At one home, he was impressed that "no one sat down at the table without offering thanks….Night and morning the head of the household read a few chapters of the Bible…singing psalms."

Portier crossed paths with a Methodist exhorter, an Anabaptist and a Presbyterian. A week into his journey, he was traveling through the Uchee and Holmes Valley area and noting the geographical wonders, featuring a "canopy of verdure, streams, springs, lakes…[and] glowing white sandy soil." If he encountered prejudice toward the Catholic faith in his traveling companions, he usually won them over by assuaging their ignorance. He also found an overwhelming sense of thankfulness for his mission, which resulted in an Irishman offering him a plot of land on which to build a church.

Presbyterian churches remained small during the territorial period, as congregants wanted well-trained and college-educated ministers. Florida's oldest organized Presbyterian church is the Euchee Valley Presbyterian Church. The church was organized in 1828 in the town of Argyle, and Scotch Presbyterians settled here among the Euchee Indian tribe. A log church at this location was replaced in 1848, and the third and current church was built in 1923. The cemetery contains the remains of many original settlers.

In 1941, Edgar Legare Pennington, rector of the Church of the Holy Cross in Miami, wrote a historical article, "The Episcopal Church in South Florida 1764–1892," detailing the Right Reverend John Young's travels throughout Florida. Pennington begins with a brief history of the seven original parishes and continues through the division of the diocese in 1892, noting at the time that "one worshipped God with no thought of the denomination." In 1867, John Freeman Young became the second bishop of Florida and started many new missions across the state, traveling on horseback, in buggies and sometimes on foot. In 1868, Young left Tallahassee to take a steamer for Key West, wanting to see the southern portion of his diocese. Getting to Key West was no small feat. He traveled four days by ship from St. Marks to Tampa and then continued to Key West, arriving the next day. His trip took almost a week, and he had to leave on the next steamer, since it only made the trip twice a month. He returned a year later.

Based on Young's journal, Pennington details the hardships and triumphs of Young's journeys: visiting Palatka before railroads made it to the area, staying with Colonial Titus long before the area was named Titusville and sailing on to New Smyrna, preaching and baptizing along the way. He often traveled with a fellow minister, and this helped keep his spirits high when recounting near disasters they faced along the way. Once, late in the day as it was getting dark, the wind died down as they were sailing, forcing them to sleep on the boat in the cold rain in Mosquito Lagoon with no warm food. He noticed on a trip to Mellonville, now Sanford—by way of Enterprise and other towns throughout the state, such as Orlando, Port Orange, Daytona, Cocoa, Eau Gallie, Leesburg, Orlando, Maitland and Palma Sola—that church building was growing across the state.

Building a church starts with community, and community churches have long been a cornerstone of the foundation for rural areas. Churches were being established from Pensacola to Key West. Baptists were predominant in rural areas, where circuit-riding preachers supplied the pulpit and often shared it with Methodists. Some Episcopal ministers traveled to seasonal churches as tourists began to enjoy the benefits of a Florida winter. People with common spiritual guidance gathered and met wherever they could, maybe in a home or newly constructed store or schoolhouse, or simply outdoors. As communities grew, each denomination would separate to form a congregation, eventually building its own church. For wealthier congregations, the simple elegance of the Greek Revival style of architecture was a popular choice from the 1820s to the 1860s. In rural Florida, simple wooden churches met the needs of new congregations. Meetinghouses could be used by any circuit rider in the 1830s, as they were shared with other denominations. Lonely rides on horseback were worth it for the preacher as he delivered the gospel, officiated marriages and conducted funerals. He comforted the sick while bringing news and entertainment. Camp meetings and revivals with tents and food might last for days, and dinner on the grounds was a social occasion.

The Methodist Church in Tallahassee started as a mission in 1824 as preachers made a circuit stop there, but one of the oldest public buildings in Tallahassee is the First Presbyterian Church, which is still used today. Construction began on the classically influenced design in 1835 and was completed in 1838. The building also was used as a place of refuge for women and children during the Seminole Wars. The church was remodeled many times from 1851 until recently, and around 1892, Gothic pointed arch windows were installed. In the 1930s, the steeple was replaced and the original bell was put in place. The first of three Trinity Methodist Churches was built in 1840. It was destroyed in 1892 to make way for the second church, a red brick semi-Gothic sanctuary constructed in 1893. That was replaced in 1962 with the most recent church.

Rustic community churches provided shelter from both the elements and battles. During the Second Seminole War (1835–42), those attending a church such as Waukeenah Methodist Church in Jefferson County would be segregated by men and women, who were divided by a wooden pole inserted into a slot in the middle of a log bench. Men carried loaded firearms and prepared for attacks, ready to take a shot from a shuttered window.

Richard Johnson Mays, a circuit rider, began preaching in 1832, although he wasn't ordained until 1841. Mays is credited with building at least six Baptist churches, and he helped found the Florida Baptist Convention. He is buried at Concord Baptist Church (a.k.a. Concord Missionary Baptist Church) on a hill in the Greenville countryside of Madison County, in the now-vanished community of Concord.

Early preachers often shared churches, and Baptist preacher Mays may have held services at the First Presbyterian Church in Monticello. It was built in the Greek Revival style using native wood, with the bricks hauled by oxcarts from South Carolina. Though a fire destroyed the church, most of the original glass windowpanes survived, according to the church website, and the church was rebuilt in 1866. The cone-shaped steeple on a square pedestal houses the five one-hundred-pound bells installed in 1882.

In 1885, the Methodist Florida Conference asked John Cole Ley to record his personal story for the *Wesleyan Christian Advocate*. Ley was born

Top: Trinity Methodist Church is shown on the left and the First Presbyterian Church is in the background, Tallahassee, circa 1910. *Courtesy of the State Archives of Florida.*

Bottom: First Presbyterian Church, Tallahassee, Leon County, circa 1870. *Courtesy of the State Archives of Florida.*

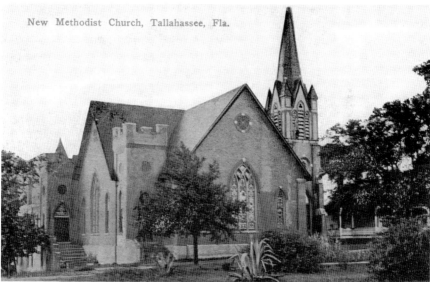

Top: The first Trinity Methodist Church (photo circa 1860), Tallahassee, Leon County. *Courtesy of the State Archives of Florida.*

Bottom: The second Trinity Methodist Church (photo circa 1900), Tallahassee, Leon County. The red brick semi-Gothic sanctuary was constructed in 1893 and replaced in 1962. *Courtesy of the State Archives of Florida.*

in Georgia in 1822 and was licensed to preach in 1843. Published in 1899, Ley's book *Fifty-Two Years in Florida* begins with a history of the state and the Methodist Church in Florida. He starts by asking that "the critic deal gently with an old man, whose life has been spent talking not writing," begging the reader to remember that the preservation of facts has been his object. He concludes with:

> *And now, dear reader, we approach the end of this humble volume. Should you say, "I am not satisfied with its contents," the author will reply in advance, "Neither am I." It has been written mostly while traveling circuits which required much riding, some of the time from necessity, to give part of my time to answering the questions for myself and family, "What shall we eat, what shall we drink, and wherewithal shall we be clothed?" leaving no means for traveling in search of records, and but little for the purchase of books for reference.*

Ley writes of his experiences and feelings but also shares the stories of others, such as the one told to him by fellow minister John L. Jerry when he was sent to St. Augustine.

> *From St. Augustine to Cowford (Jacksonville), forty miles, he traveled without seeing a house; from thence to Newmansville, sixty-five miles, by Indian trail; thence to Micanopy, thirty miles, etc. These lonely rides made on horseback, carrying his clothes, books, lunch, and a little sack of corn to feed his horse. He told me that during one of these lonely rides, his money reduced to less than one dollar, he stopped to lunch and feed his horse. Feeling deeply depressed, he went to a cluster of bushes to pray. Seeing something glitter in the sunshine and supposing it was a button dropped by some Cavalier of the olden time, he thought he would go and pick it up as a relic. But what was his surprise when, on taking it in his hand, he found it a Spanish doubloon ($16). This met all his wants until Quarterly Conference, when he received his installment of missionary money. Beyond this, it established in his mind that faith in God's special promises which he never lost.*

Ley recounts that in his 1845 visit to Fort Call, there were no church buildings, but the settlers opened their doors, neighbors came together and later, they *built at Fort Call a church of pine poles, and hewed puncheons for floor and seats. We sawed-out doors and windows, made a rude table, and the building was complete. It would doubtless have compared poorly to St. Peter's.*

Ley spent four years in Key West supporting the Cuban Mission and was happy to see the dedication of the people to move into their own premises. The house in which they worshipped was neat and capable of seating three hundred people but "not altogether such a one as we could have desired." The worshippers made plans to build a church, a cornerstone was laid and stone was quarried from the island for three years. They raised money and paid for the construction as it was completed, so as not to incur debt. When the walls of the first story were done, they secured a temporary cover and began worshiping in the church building. It was later finished as a one-story building.

Other creative houses of worship in which Ley visited included a small U.S. garrison house in Tampa, in 1846; by 1899, the congregation had a church building. A log house, which was also the courthouse, theater and dancing hall, was used in Ocala before a beautiful church was built in 1899. And Palatka worshippers met in an old government building until a "pretty and commodious church" was built in 1884. On Cedar Key, the community shared a school basement with the Presbyterians and the Baptists until they could build their own church. When the railroad bypassed them on the way to Tampa, closing mills, and a damaging storm swept through, the population went into sharp decline. Ley felt a fondness for the Florida pioneers and shared this:

I cannot leave this part of the subject without a word of commendation to the kind pioneers of East Florida at that day. There was nothing in their power too good for God's ministers. The best they could command they set before him; and would often walk miles, wading through water, for their preacher to walk across a swollen stream upon a fallen log, then take his horse and swim it over, and, meeting the parson on the other shore, would shake his hand and send him dry to his next appointment.

Originally known as Methodist Episcopal Church at Black Creek, the Middleburg United Methodist Church was founded in 1828 by Isaac Boring. Boring was a Methodist circuit rider who traveled at times along the Bellamy Road to reach his towns. He made stops in St. Augustine, Fernandina, Jacksonville, Palatka, Gainesville, Lake City and Micanopy. This frame

Middleburg United Methodist Church, a.k.a Methodist Episcopal Church at Black Creek, Middleburg, Clay County, circa 1880s. *Courtesy of the State Archives of Florida.*

vernacular building is the oldest Methodist church in Florida, built around 1847, and Middleburg United Methodist Church is still in use today. A bell tower was added in 1852 and a church bell installed in 1860.

Born in South Carolina in 1818, Methodist Reverend Simon Peter Richardson left an almost three-hundred-page autobiography covering nearly sixty years of his life before he died in 1899. In *The Light and Shadows of Itinerant Life: An Autobiography of Reverend Simon Peter Richardson*, he writes, "The first year of my itinerant life was one of more shadows than lights." His unique personality comes across: a humorous, philosophical, devout Methodist Christian and fascinating storyteller. Richardson worked the Jacksonville circuit of more than two hundred miles for twenty years. He traveled from southern Georgia throughout northeast Florida and later recalled the events of his years of service as an itinerant minister in pioneer Florida, when "for 3 years my saddlebag had been my wardrobe and library." John B. Robins writes in the introduction: "Many a sad heart has been made bright by his words. He went through this life scattering joy and sunshine along his pathway, respected by old and young, and loved by all. He possessed wit of a high order, and sarcasm that was like a consuming fire." Nearly all preachers of that day traveled on horseback and moved their families in covered wagons.

The Methodist Church and its preachers at the time were much opposed to written or read sermons, yet Richardson would write and rewrite his sermons. He noted, "Don't try to read and preach at the same time. If you read, read; and if you preach, preach." Illness, poverty, hunger and danger did not stop his mission. Richardson felt a calling from God and reminded himself that "He appointed me to take care of myself, and when my strength fails then the Lord will do the rest." Jacksonville was then only a village, located on the north side of the St. Johns River, just beginning to get noticed as a resort for invalids from the northern part of the United States and tourists soon followed. The circuit extended to King's Ferry on the St. Mary's River, the dividing line between Georgia and Florida.

In 1844, there was no Methodist church in St. Augustine, so Richardson secured a lot and contracted to have a church built. He noted, "The old cathedral was still standing there, with a cement floor and chime of bells." Richardson was later appointed to the Key West Station and found he was the only regular preacher on the island, although there were several church buildings: Catholic, Episcopal, Baptist and Presbyterian. Much to his dismay, he commented, "At the time there were 32 grog shops." Ten years later, when Richardson worked for the American Bible Society, he traveled to Key West and arrived to a welcoming reunion. He traveled across the Panhandle from Jacksonville to Pensacola, impressed by the magnificent bay and the locals. "There I saw for the first time a man who had been working under the water in a submarine armor. I saw the large diving-bell, and was invited to take a seat in it, but I got scared and backed out."

The congregation of Pisgah Church in Tallahassee was at one time ministered to by circuit-riding preachers. A new church was built in 1859

Pisgah United Methodist Church, Tallahassee, Leon County, 1924. *Courtesy of the State Archives of Florida.*

and dedicated by the Reverend Richardson. The three front-door entrances were used, as men sat on one side and women on the other and slaves were required to sit in the gallery. Before the end of the Seminole Wars, armed men stood guard outside against attacks. Confederate soldiers and 1841 yellow fever epidemic victims are buried in the cemetery at this church.

In 1926, historical writer Susan Branch Bradford Eppes recounted a sermon from a West Virginia circuit preacher in her work *Through Some Eventful Years*. He had preached earlier at Pisgah but made some unwelcome remarks. Not wishing to condemn him, a large congregation gathered at Mount Zion to hear him.

> *He had been on the circuit for years and at every home in the neighborhood he and his family had been entertained, sometimes for weeks….In the event of a lengthy visit, a nurse was provided for the children….The family seamstress was at her disposal…with an account at every store in Tallahassee. We had heard he had made some unwelcome remarks in the pulpit at Pisgah. Gathered at Mount Zion anxious to hear him preach…. Each had come ready to supply a liberal addition to "the plate" when it should be passed. Then the pastor quoted Mark 10:25. "It is easier for a camel to go through the eye of a needle than for a rich man to enter the kingdom of God." He preached on the danger of riches and the evil effect with ultimate damnation, the lengthy sermon was the last for him at Mount Zion.*

Another glimpse into the life of a circuit rider comes from Jeremiah Rast, a Methodist Episcopal from South Carolina who describes his Florida journeys in *Life Sketches—Striking Incidents and Sermons*. In the preface to the book, L.W. Moore writes: "He makes no pretensions to literary merits; all he aims at is to state some of the precious and startling things of his four score years as a fully sanctified man and local Preacher." An abusive teacher prompted Rast to drop out of school at an early age. Education was still important to him, so he did what he could to learn on his own. After a circuit rider came to his hometown, Rast felt the call to share the gospel and applied for a license to exhort, which was the first step toward becoming a lay preacher. He describes his "religious awakening" of 1843: "When I laid down on my bed that night there seemed to be a lovely light shining on me. With the impression that it was the light of Heaven in that condition I dropped to sleep, and it was the sweetest night's sleep that I ever remembered to have had in my life." Rast moved to Orange

The First Baptist Church of Citra, Marion County, north of Ocala on US 301
Author's collection.

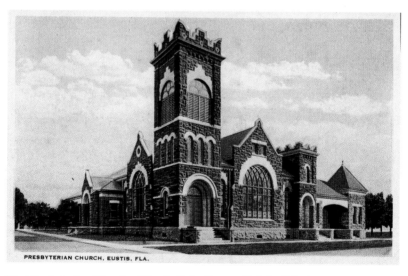

PRESBYTERIAN CHURCH, EUSTIS, FLA.

First Presbyterian Church of Eustis, Lake County. Built by E.L. Ferran with bricks textured to resemble granite. Photo circa 1914. *Courtesy of the State Archives of Florida.*

Congregational Church on Washington Street.   New Smyrna, Fla.

First Methodist Church, Tampa, Fla.

Above: Christ Congregational Church, New Smyrna, built in 1889, had stained-glass windows that were removed and installed in the new Christ Church built across the street. Photo circa 1900. *Courtesy of the State Archives of Florida.*

Left: The First Methodist Church, Tampa, was built in 1853. The spire atop the steeple was a downtown landmark. The church was razed and replaced in the 1960s. Photo circa 1909. *Courtesy of the State Archives of Florida.*

Plaza de la Constitution and Cathedral of St. Augustine, circa 1907. *Courtesy of the State Archives of Florida.*

The Ancient Spanish Shrine of Nuestra Senora de la Leche, St. Augustine, Florida, circa 1956. *Courtesy of the State Archives of Florida.*

CHAPEL, FORT MARION, ST. AUGUSTINE, FLA.

St. Johns Episcopal Church, Jacksonville, Fla.

This page, top: Catholic Chapel at Castillo de San Marcos, St. Augustine, St. Johns County, circa 1911. *Courtesy of the State Archives of Florida.*

This page, bottom: St. John's Cathedral, a.k.a St. John's Episcopal Church, Jacksonville, Duval County, circa 1909. *Courtesy of the State Archives of Florida.*

Opposite, top: Moss Hill Methodist Church, Vernon, Washington County. *Courtesy of Pat and Carolyn Sheffield.*

Opposite, bottom: Falling Creek United Methodist Church, Lake City, Columbia County. *Author's collection.*

Top: LaGrange
Community
Church, Mims,
Brevard County.
Author's collection.

Bottom: First United
Methodist Church,
Bagdad, Santa
Rosa County.
Author's collection.

St. Luke's Episcopal Church of Courtenay, Merritt Island, Brevard County. *Author's collection.*

St. Andrews Episcopal Church, a.k.a Old St. Andrews, Jacksonville, Duval County, circa 1900. *Courtesy of the State Archives of Florida.*

Robert Sands Schuyler–
designed churches: St.
Mark's Episcopal Church,
a.k.a All Saints Episcopal
Church, Starke, Bradford
County (*this page, top*);
St. George Episcopal
Church, Fort George
Island, Duval County
(*this page, bottom*); Beaches
Museum Chapel, a.k.a
St Paul's By-the-Sea,
Jacksonville Beach, Duval
County (*opposite, top*);
Grace Church, Orange
Park, Clay County, circa
1880 (*opposite, bottom*).
*Author's collection and State
Archives of Florida.*

Above: St. Paul's Episcopal Church, Federal Point, Putnam County. *Author's collection.*

Left: Wacahoota United Methodist, near Williston, Levy County. *Author's collection.*

Opposite, top: Port Tampa United Methodist Church, Tampa, Hillsborough County. *Author's collection.*

Opposite, bottom: Sacred Heart Catholic Church, a.k.a St. Louis Catholic Church, Tampa, Hillsborough County, circa 1909. *Courtesy of the State Archives of Florida.*

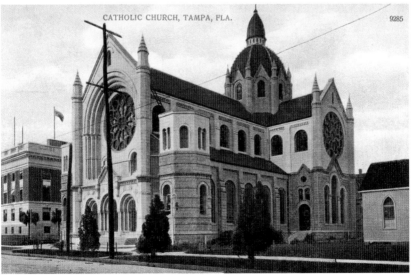

CATHOLIC CHURCH, TAMPA, FLA.   9285

GRACE METHODIST EPISCOPAL CHURCH, ST. AUGUSTINE, FLA.

MEMORIAL (PRESBYTERIAN) CHURCH, ST. AUGUSTINE, FLA.

A-13537

Three churches built by Henry Flagler in St. Augustine, St. Johns County: Grace United Methodist Church, circa 1923 (*this page, top*); Memorial Presbyterian Church, a.k.a Flagler Memorial Church, circa 1900 (*this page, bottom*); Ancient City Baptist Church, circa 1911 (*opposite*). *Photos courtesy of the State Archives of Florida.*

Ancient City Baptist Church,
St. Augustine, Fla.

Replica of the original St. John's Episcopal Church with the bell tower at Pioneer Village at Shingle Creek and the original church as it looks today, Kissimmee, Osceola County. *Author's collection.*

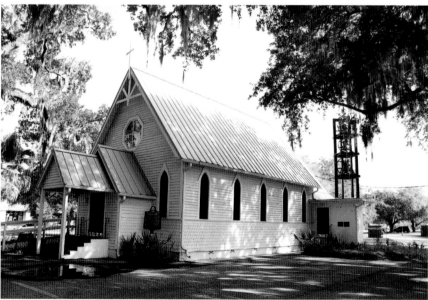

Right: Homeland Methodist Church, Homeland Heritage Park, Polk County. *Author's collection.*

Below: Former St. Rita's Catholic Church Mission, now Mary S. Harrell Black Heritage Museum, New Smyrna Beach, Volusia County. *Author's collection.*

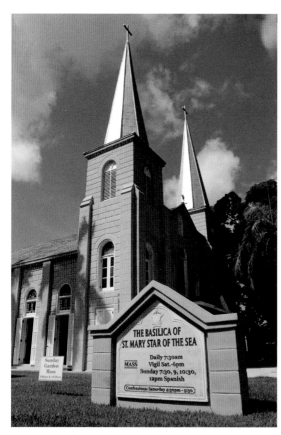

Left: Basilica of St. Mary Star of the Sea, Key West, Monroe County. *Author's collection.*

Below: Moss Hill Methodist Church, Vernon, Washington County. *Courtesy of Pat and Carolyn Sheffield.*

Orange Springs Methodist Episcopal Church, Marion County. *Author's collection.*

Springs in Marion County in 1857, and from there his ministry continued until 1876, covering an area across Central Florida from Nassau County to Cedar Key, including Ocala, Micanopy and Middleburg. Among his many stories, he shares the time when he was called on to marry a couple in 1870. At the end of supper, they brought out a glass of "Sillabub." The host assured Rast there was nothing intoxicating in it, just milk and eggs and sugar and spice, yet by the time the guests started for home, there was much laughing and talking and shouting. Having had a glass or two, Rast decided it best he just stop talking.

Orange Springs Methodist Episcopal Church, built in 1852, was served by circuit riders. Available to all denominations, it was also home to church socials, camp meetings, concerts and political debates. The cemetery features gravestones dating to 1853. The doors and windows were made in Palatka and transported by steamboat, but the church building was constructed of locally milled lumber. The church is the only structure remaining from when the town was platted by the founder, John W. Pearson. He donated the property for the church and cemetery, as well as materials for construction of the church using local labor.

When Orange Springs was platted in 1853, eighty city blocks and twenty streets were planned. Visitors came by stagecoach to the once-popular winter tourist attraction, seeking the benefits and beauty of Florida's crystal-clear spring water. The town was also home to a private school for girls housed at the local hotel. Then the railroad built to the north rerouted tourists, and the town and the church suffered. When Episcopal Bishop John F. Young visited in 1868, the church was boarded up. Repairs began in the mid 1920s, and a porch was added in the 1960s.

The Reverend William Penn McEwen, a Methodist, and the Reverend John W. Hendry, a Methodist turned Baptist, shared the circuit throughout old Manatee County when it covered a larger portion of Florida, including today's Hardee and DeSoto Counties. They often shared responsibilities at the pulpit, covering for each other especially in times of crisis. On occasion, the denominations met together with a shared message. Settlers traveled miles on horseback or horse and buggy, down cow paths and through rivers and streams, just to hear the word of God from godly men. Railroads would soon become a popular mode of transportation.

Hendry was born in Georgia in 1836 and moved to Florida in 1848. His Methodist faith was challenged when he did an intense study of the Bible and came to feel the Baptist church more closely followed his beliefs, but he still believed "winning souls was far more important than denominations." So when Methodist preacher McEwen, who was also born in Georgia, arrived in the area in 1867, they traveled together over the same roads and preached from the same pulpits, filling in for each other when necessary.

Chapter 4

CARPENTER CABIN
TO GOTHIC CATHEDRAL

It takes all sorts to make a world; or a church.
—*C.S. Lewis,* Letters to Malcolm: Chiefly on Prayer

The Civil War left people impoverished, both financially and spiritually. Many churches were burned, abandoned or neglected, and church growth slowed to almost a standstill. The Reconstruction period in Florida sparked renewed growth. Unpaved roads were carved out of the wilderness by heavy wagonloads of supplies and settlers. The virgin forests of the 1850s and 1860s had been cleared to make way for plantations. Left abandoned after the Civil War, these areas were platted for towns, and postwar growth brought visitors from the North to come and enjoy the state's natural resources along with its beauty and mild climate. From simple log cabins to elaborate cathedrals, the many architectural styles found in Florida in the late 1800s reflect a diverse past.

Log structures started to disappear. At Falling Creek United Methodist Church in Lake City, a wood clapboard building replaced the original log cabin built when the church was first established in the 1850s. As noted on an informational sign, the church is located "up the road" from Falling Creek Falls and Park. The church features two front doors, one for men and one for women—they sat on opposite sides of the church. According to a plaque at the church, the Baptists worshipped there until 1866.

In 1872 near Titusville at Mims, LaGrange Community Church, a frame vernacular church, was built, with horizontal boards placed over the original vertical logs. The first floor was home to the church, while the second floor housed the first schoolhouse in Brevard County. It also served as a community center. The second story was removed in 1893, and the remodeling included adding a bell tower. Although it served as a Baptist church until 1953, Episcopals, Methodists and Presbyterians also held services there. Many would travel on Saturday to attend church on Sunday morning, often followed by dinner on the grounds and another service in the late afternoon. From inside the church, you can more clearly see the etchings on the pointed colored-glass windows that feature the names and dates of those who helped build the church.

Rivers carried people, mail, supplies and visitors to the many towns and communities that sprung up along the way. Some wanted a seasonal place to worship in keeping with their elaborate lifestyle, while settlers simply wanted a sense of community. These evolving lifestyles brought about a change in the architecture for homes and churches. Long before electricity and indoor plumbing, churches, schools, newspaper offices, general stores and libraries were becoming a part of everyday life in Florida. Citrus groves and sawmills brought industry as Floridians pushed further south. Gristmills and ferry services at the river's edge prompted the growth of towns and communities and an interest in exploring the more remote regions of the state. Bishop Young established mission churches after the Civil War devastation, and many of these churches can still be seen along the St. Johns River. Communities began to grow and thrive thanks to the ease of travel by steamboat.

During the Reconstruction period, some churches were built in the Neo-Gothic style while others maintained a more modest approach, resulting in a flurry of simple wooden churches. Churches were home to poor Floridians as well as wealthy Victorian-era tourists who traveled south to enjoy the winters in Florida. Many of the most charming Carpenter Gothic churches dot the shores of the meandering St. Johns River and are some of the most picturesque in the state. Graceful Gothic designs expressed in wood are what make Carpenter Gothic churches so beautiful, as shown by the unique building style and use of available materials. From islands to inland, many are still standing today.

Writers have been drawn to the unique beauty of these Florida churches when storytelling. Retired architect Charles E. Pattillo III was inspired to self-publish *St. Dunstan's & John* in 2008, and his fictional tale begins with a discussion of many of the Carpenter Gothic churches along or near the St. Johns River. Eugenia Price wrote about St. Margaret's Episcopal Church as part of the novel *Margaret's Story*, which is the last book in a trilogy of

St. Margaret's Episcopal Church, Hibernia, Clay County, circa 1903. *Courtesy of the State Archives of Florida.*

historical novels set in St. Augustine. Price tells a fictional story about real-life Margaret Seton Fleming and her family at home on Hibernia Plantation on Fleming Island, located along the western bank of the St. Johns River between Green Cove Springs and Orange Park. The property, built by Irish immigrant George Fleming in 1790, was passed along to his son, Colonel Lewis Michael Fleming, who married Margaret Seton soon after his first wife died.

With the help of Bishop Young, Margaret Seton Fleming was instrumental in planning and building St. Margaret's Episcopal Church in 1875. The Carpenter Gothic–style church is named in honor of Saint Margaret of Scotland, homeland of the Seton family. Construction began with the backing of Margaret Fleming and the help of Bishop Young. One of the first services held in the unfinished chapel was for Margaret Fleming's funeral in 1878. In 1880, the chapel was relocated to its current location and is nearly hidden down a dirt road. Hibernia was named after the Latin word for Ireland, homeland of the Flemings. Charles Seton, Margaret's father, was the first mayor of Fernandina, and Francis Philip Fleming, son of Margaret and Lewis, went on to become the fifteenth governor of Florida.

Gothic Revival architecture with a medieval flair rose in popularity during the first half of the 1800s (1830s–60s). Notable features included steeply pitched roofs, gingerbread trim, pointed arch windows with tracery and colored glass. Victorian Gothic architecture (1860–90) showcases a variety of colors and textures. The impetus to construct so many Carpenter Gothic churches in Florida started with one man, Richard Upjohn.

The American Gothic architect Upjohn designed Trinity Episcopal Church in New York City. After the success of his building style, requests for his architectural plans poured into his office. He resolved to publish a book, mostly for small or poor parishes, illustrating churches he had designed and could recommend for parishes in need of correct but inexpensive models. Upjohn felt that, as an expression of his faith, it was his duty to supply his Carpenter Gothic designs at little or no cost to small parishes. He wrote *Rural Architecture* in 1852. Using inexpensive local materials and locally skilled labor, he provided a basis for individual design on a small budget, with simple artistic construction resulting in small wood-frame structures with all the essential features of a church. His brilliance is reflected in the many Carpenter Gothic–style churches scattered across the landscape of Florida. Each is unique and reflects the diverse communities in which it was built.

Although the first Jewish temple in Florida was organized after the Civil War in Pensacola, one Carpenter Gothic building was home to the United Hebrews of Ocala Temple, the first Hebrew synagogue in Ocala. Located in the Tuscawilla Park Historic District, it later became the Ocala Bible Chapel. It is now home to another Christian congregation. The simplicity found in what was once the Hebrew synagogue in Ocala shows a basic Carpenter Gothic style compared to the more elaborate St. Mary's Church built in Green Cove Springs in the late 1870s.

Green Cove Springs, at one time called Magnolia, was referred to as the "Saratoga of the South." Wealthy Northerners came for "taking the water," meaning to soak in or drink water from mineral springs. That practice had long been thought to have healing powers. St. Mary's Episcopal Church in Green Cove Springs has been described as one of the best examples of the Carpenter Gothic style in Florida. Its board-and-batten siding, steep gable roof, lancet windows and tall spire are all classic traits of Carpenter Gothic architecture. Located about forty feet from the St. Johns River, it was built on piers to prevent flooding. Panels under the lancet windows help with ventilation, and pews are equipped with a fire escape door in the wall. Its triangular battens cover the vertical siding board seams. Built in 1879, a bell tower was added in 1880.

St. Mary's Episcopal Church was built as a mission church, meaning it was financially dependent, as opposed to a self-sufficient parish church. Many of Florida's historic wooden churches reflect some elements of Carpenter Gothic design, while others serve as a reminder of the simplicity of living in

United Hebrews of Ocala Temple, a.k.a Temple B'nai Darom, Ocala, Marion County, circa 1888. *Courtesy of the State Archives of Florida.*

an isolated pioneer community. Just as stone Gothic Revival churches were influenced by the notion that materials used should reflect construction, so too were Carpenter Gothic churches of pioneer Florida. The transformation of stone pattern to wood is what makes these artistic gems so unique.

Carpenter Gothic designs were readily adaptable to the environment, adding beauty and grace, while using local carpenters or laymen to do much of the work. Stone features were fabricated in native hardwoods with locally milled lumber. Wood frames were often built of old-growth pine with easily installed board-and-batten siding, where planks are placed vertically, and their joints are covered with thin strips of wood, or a combination of narrow and wide strips of wood is used to cover seams. Common architectural features often included decorative verge-board or barge-board trim (sometimes called gingerbread trim); lancet (narrow, pointed) windows; stained-glass windows that sometimes tell a story; steeply pitched roofs with

St. Mary's Episcopal Church, Green Cove Springs, Clay County, circa 1936. *Courtesy of the State Archives of Florida.*

gables; and a bell cote if there is no belfry. A bell cote is the small external housing mounted on a roof peak over the main entrance. A belfry is the part of the steeple that houses the bell or bells in a semi-enclosed space.

In 1870, Henry Shelton Sanford purchased over twelve thousand acres of land west of Mellonville to found the community of Sanford. In 1877,

SANFORD CHURCHES

First Presbyterian Church

REV. J. F. McKINNON
Pastor First Presbyterian Church

First Methodist Church

REV. GEORGE B. WALDRON
Pastor Congregational Church

REV. A. E. HOUSHOLDER
Pastor Methodist Episcopal Church

First Baptist Church

REV. J. W. WILDMAN
Pastor First Baptist Church

Church of the Holy Cross, Episcopal

Church, Catholic

A FEW OF THE QUARTETTE OF

REV. B. F. BROWN
Rector Holy Cross Episcopal Church

Churches and ministers of the past in Sanford, Seminole County: Reverends J.F. McKinnon, George B. Waldron, A.E. Housholdes, J.W. Wildman and B.F. Brown, circa 1910. *Courtesy of the State Archives of Florida.*

Sanford was incorporated with eight churches in the area, and Mellonville became a part of Sanford in 1883. Holy Cross Episcopal, also known as the Church of the Holy Cross of Sanford, built in 1873, was an original Richard Upjohn design and a gift from Henry Sanford to the town of Sanford. It was consecrated by Bishop Young. The church was destroyed by a hurricane in 1880 and rebuilt on a modified Upjohn plan in which the church spire could be seen from the nearby St. Johns River. That church was destroyed by fire in 1923. The third church, built in the Spanish style, stands today near downtown Sanford. Other churches built or rebuilt nearby include a Catholic, a Presbyterian, a Methodist and a Baptist church.

Enterprise was the last port of call along the St. Johns River, welcoming steamships and paddleboats carrying parishioners and priests to the area.

All Saints Church Enterprise and rectory, circa 1900. *Courtesy of the State Archives of Florida.*

According to the website for All Saints Episcopal Church in Enterprise, the vicar of Holy Cross Episcopal Church, Sanford, rowed across Lake Monroe to conduct services in the parlor of the Brock House, a winter resort for wealthy northern visitors. Jacob Brock built the Brock House, and later, he and Count Frederick DeBary donated money to the building of a church. Two years later, in 1883, the community of worshippers built a church on land donated by Lester Clark located on Clark Street. Made of local cypress and pine, with board-and-batten siding and pointed arch windows, All Saints Episcopal Church Enterprise reflects the Carpenter Gothic style. At one time, the church was enclosed by a white picket fence. In 1950, a small sacristy was added to the back of the church, and in 1971, a ramp and front porch were added.

Another church along the St. Johns River was founded in Mandarin and built with the help of famed author Harriet Beecher Stowe. At that time, Stowe was a recent convert to the Episcopal Church and a winter resident of Mandarin. In a letter to her brother Charles Beecher, she shared her desire to build a church in her Florida community. She "had a longing to be more immediately doing Christ's work on earth." The process began by contacting the bishop of Florida. Charles wrote that "through her efforts, Mandarin had been provided with a pretty little Episcopal church." Completed in 1883, the Episcopal Church of Our Savior was destroyed by a hurricane in 1964, and a new church was built in 1967. Harriet Beecher Stowe is best known for her novel *Uncle Tom's Cabin*, but she also wrote beautiful Florida sketches about her life in Mandarin called *Palmetto Leaves*.

Episcopal Church of Our Savior, Mandarin, Duval County, 1953. *Courtesy of the State Archives of Florida.*

Built in 1885 with lumber from the local Bagdad mills, the First United Methodist Church of Bagdad suffered damage from fire and hurricanes, only to be rebuilt. The beauty of the shiplap siding (one board partly overlaps the next board) secured with square-cut nails and the delicate woodwork around the porch and eaves give this little white church a storybook feel. It is in the small former lumber mill community of Bagdad in Northwest Florida near the Blackwater River. Another local church nearby is the New Providence Missionary Baptist Church, now home to the Bagdad Museum. Built in the 1880s, it was moved to its current location in 1980s.

Bishop Young was so dedicated to his endeavor to build beautiful little churches that he often took matters into his own hands by selecting and clearing the sites. He used an ax in a wooded area along the Indian River to help clear the site for St. Mark's Episcopal Church, Cocoa. The altar windows were placed as a memorial to him. An earlier Episcopal address describes this simple board-and-batten church built in 1886 as "a perfect gem and in every way adapted to the position which it occupies by the side of the water amid palm trees." Today much of the original church has been remodeled to keep

St. Mark's Episcopal Church, Cocoa, Brevard County, circa 1900. *Courtesy of the State Archives of Florida.*

up with the needs of an ever-growing parish, which now includes a school. The increasing population of an area can sometimes outpace the capacity of a church but can contribute to a unique style when remodeling. Today the exterior of the church has been changed to a Spanish style.

Constructed in 1888, St. Luke's Episcopal Church of Courtenay is a simple Carpenter Gothic–style church on Merritt Island. Built of locally milled island pine and cypress, it sits among lovely oaks near the Indian River Lagoon and is surrounded on three sides by an old cemetery. The charming setting isn't far from rocket launches and throngs of tourists enjoying the coastal waterways of nearby lagoons and rivers.

It wasn't only the Episcopal faith that eagerly built new churches. The first two churches built in Mount Dora were a Methodist and a Congregational church. The Methodist church was torn down in 1940, and a new church was built, but the bell was saved. The Congregational Church of Mt. Dora is possibly the oldest building in town, built around 1894. This Victorian revival–style wood-frame church was attended by President and Mrs. Calvin Coolidge while they were staying at the nearby Lakeside Inn.

Renowned architect and devout Episcopalian Robert Sands Schuyler designed several Gothic Revival and Carpenter Gothic–style churches after moving to Florida in 1878. The church he designed in Waldo was demolished, but some of his other original designs are still standing. St. Mark's Episcopal Church was originally in Fairbanks but later moved to Starke. Schuyler's architectural skills are on full display in the St. George Episcopal Church on Fort George Island. Other churches he designed include St. Paul's By-the-Sea in Jacksonville Beach; St. Andrew's Church in Jacksonville; St. Peter's Episcopal Church in Fernandina Beach, considered an architectural gem; and Grace Church in Orange Park. Founded in 1880, Grace Church at Orange Park in Clay County, also designed by Schuyler (not to be confused with Grace Episcopal Church in Port Orange, Volusia County, constructed in 1893), stands today as the Episcopal Chapel, with a new church building across the street.

St. Mark's Episcopal Church, also known as All Saints Episcopal Church, was built in the 1880s. This Carpenter Gothic church was disassembled, numbered board by board and moved from Fairbanks to Starke, where it was reassembled and consecrated in 1902. Stained-glass windows were

THE FIRST TWO CHURCHES

Methodist 1885

5th & Baker
(Sunoco Station now on site)

Congregational 1887

Corner 7th & Donnelly

PLATE XXIV

First two churches in Mount Dora, Methodist Church and Congregational Church, Lake County, circa 1880. *Courtesy of the State Archives of Florida.*

added later. The Parish House opened in 1942 as a joint church service center with the Presbyterians for soldiers at Camp Blanding seeking the comforts of home.

In 1877, a group of Episcopalians met with Bishop Young and established a mission on Fort George Island. At that time, the barrier island was accessible only by boat. Plans were made to build a church. In 1881, before the windows were completed, the openings were covered with canvas so services could be held inside. Two years, later in 1883, stained-glass windows were installed in St. George Episcopal Church. One window depicts St. George, patron saint of England, as a young knight slaying his dragon. The 1937 paper "A Works Progress Administration Church Record for Saint George's Church" provides a story about St. George's mission, written by Lee Eugene Bigelow: "The little chapel of St. George's is today just as it was when first completed." In reference to the church bell, he recounts from a pastor's 1884 letter: "The bell had just been procured and hung, so of course, we had to try it; and sweetly will it sound through the crispy air next winter, calling worshippers far and near."

St. Paul's By-the-Sea was moved several times before finding a permanent home on Jacksonville Beach as the deconsecrated Beaches Chapel. This 1887 church designed by Robert Sands Schuyler was built two blocks from where it stands now as part of the Pablo Historical Park and Beaches Museum. It was moved from Pablo Beach (now Jacksonville Beach) inland, then turned; it was later split in half and enlarged and the bell tower was removed. Relocated again with a name change to Beaches Chapel in 2012, it was moved to Pablo Historical Park. The stained-glass windows are not original.

The King's Handbook of Notable Episcopal Churches in the US, published in 1889, includes the Schuyler-designed 1887 St. Andrew's Episcopal Church. The brick Gothic Revival–style church was dedicated in the 1880s as a tribute or memorial to the late Bishop John Freeman Young. It was one of the few buildings to survive the devastating fire in downtown Jacksonville in 1901. By the mid-1980s, it was abandoned and in a state of decay. The deconsecrated Old St. Andrew's, as it is now known, serves as an event venue under the care of the Jacksonville Historical Society.

Amelia Island churches, as many other Florida churches, each have a unique story to tell, but the jewel of the city is considered to be St. Peter's Episcopal Church. At one time, the town was called Fernandina, but the name was later changed to Fernandina Beach. The aftermath of the Civil War left St. Peter's Episcopal Church in near ruin when occupied by Federal

Left: Architectural rendering of St. Peter's Episcopal Church of Fernandina Beach, circa 1870. *Courtesy of the State Archives of Florida.*

Below: A 1910 photo of the completed church with changes to the tower, Nassau County. *Courtesy of the State Archives of Florida.*

forces. By 1881, ground had been broken for a new stone church designed by Robert Sands Schuyler. The first services were held in 1884, but the new church was heavily damaged by a fire in 1892. In 1893, Schuyler was retained to help with the rebuilding of the Neo-Gothic–style church.

St. Paul's Episcopal Church in East Palatka at Federal Point was built in 1882. Locals sold hollowed-out alligator eggs painted with scenes of Florida to northern visitors to help pay for the stained-glass windows that were added to this Carpenter Gothic church in 1883. In 1892, a bell was purchased. The serene setting welcomes worshippers today just as it did when the church was first established.

In the 1880s, citrus began to replace plantation crops as a source of revenue, and British immigrants came to Central Florida with dreams and designs to build on the citrus culture. Many churches reflected the Neo-Gothic style and replaced the simple style of earlier church designs. In 1882, Englishman Granville Chetwynd-Stapylton came to Central Florida and created the colony of Chetwynd. He established orange groves on this pioneer land and provided a learning center for workers employed at his orange grove business, Stapylton and Company. He also built a boardinghouse, dining hall

Holy Trinity Episcopal Church, Fruitland Park, (Tavares) Lake County, circa 1880. *Courtesy of the State Archives of Florida.*

and stable to help recruit well-educated single British young men to come and learn the business of growing citrus. The Carpenter Gothic church he built is all that is left of the former colony of Chetwynd. Many of the settlers moved on after the devastating freezes of 1894 and 1895 wiped out nearly all the citrus trees in Central Florida.

Holy Trinity Episcopal Church in Fruitland Park stands today much as it did on the day of the first services held in 1888 at Chetwynd. The fancy fish scale shingle–covered church originally housed a bell tower that eventually became a home for bats and a target for lightning strikes. The tower was removed in 1925. A white wooden lych-gate was added in 1889 and is said to be one of the oldest, if not the oldest, lych-gates in the country. Originally designed as a sheltered resting place for pallbearers, it is now used for the family to rest for prayers with the clergy before entering the church.

Beautiful small-town churches were still being built in the less populated areas of the state. In Fort Meade, Christ Episcopal Church looks as if it was made for a movie set—and this historic church was just that. This Carpenter Gothic–style church founded in 1886 was used in 1990 for the HBO film *Judgment*. The movie captured an ugly story, but the church still stands in glory for the charming community of Fort Meade. The pointed arch windows, gabled roofs and three-story bell tower add to its beauty. It was built by early immigrants from England, Scotland, Ireland and Wales.

The one-room sanctuary of Wacahoota United Methodist Church was used as a backdrop setting for a blue jean commercial in the 1970s. Located on Southwest Williston Road (SR 121) in Levy County, the church was built with pine floorboards and hardwood pews in 1899. According to the Florida Conference of the United Methodist Church, an annual homecoming service is held each year in November.

In 1839, Madison County commissioners set aside an area on Meeting Street (now Avenue) for three Protestant churches: Baptist, Methodist and Presbyterian. Only the Baptist church remains at the corner of Meeting Avenue and Base Street. The 1898 sanctuary of the Pioneer Hickstown Baptist Church, now the First Baptist Church of Madison, was moved one block southwest in 1956 to make way for a new sanctuary. Located at West Pickney Street and South Orange Street, the original First Baptist Church now serves as a Sunday school building. The Queen Anne–style architecture is attributed to the Reverend Stephen Crockett, an Englishman who served as pastor at the time. Crockett's design is unusual for the time and place, with an octagonal interior plan. The Reverend Richard Johnson Mays was one of the original founders.

Christ Episcopal Church, Fort Meade, Polk County, circa 1900. *Courtesy of the State Archives of Florida.*

Original First Baptist Church, Madison, Madison County, circa 1900. *Courtesy of the State Archives of Florida.*

Port Tampa is home to a church built in 1894 where Roosevelt's Rough Riders could attend before shipping off to the Spanish-American War. According to the church website, Port Tampa United Methodist Church began as a mission to the South Tampa wilderness. The church was built by Methodists from up north to provide a place of worship for railroad and dock workers in the area. It also served as a school for Port Tampa City.

The Tampa Board of Trade published a pamphlet in 1910 noting that the clergy of Tampa held a position of commanding influence.

Few cities in the South have larger representation among the religious denominations. The Roman Catholics are particularly strong and have a Cathedral which is unsurpassed in the south in architectural dignity and beauty. The Methodist, Presbyterian, Baptist, and Episcopal denominations have beautiful church homes and are strong in organization and effort. Other denominations are plentifully represented.

It started in 1859 as a small frame church named St. Louis Catholic Church, located at Florida Avenue and Twiggs Street in downtown Tampa. The city began to grow rapidly after the arrival of Henry Plant and his railroad in 1884 and, later, the Plant Hotel in 1891. The little wooden church was replaced in 1898 with a beautiful building, and its name was changed to Sacred Heart Catholic Church. The founding pastors and successors are buried in the nearby St. Louis Cemetery.

The 1800s were a period of growth for Florida. In 1884, a new state constitution replaced the one created in 1868. Railroads and truck farming were new industries, and the population grew. Resort areas were emerging throughout the state. Wealthy northern visitors came looking for rest and relaxation as hotels began to dot the East Coast. Then a devastating fire swept through St. Augustine, destroying the historic cathedral along with the St. Augustine hotel, where the fire started, and other downtown buildings. They would rebuild, and the land of orange groves and ocean breezes would soon embrace the Gilded Age (1877) and continue building beautiful cathedrals and charming churches.

Chapter 5

ALMOST FORGOTTEN CHURCHES

Education and culture can never reform a nation, it takes righteousness.
—Jeremiah Rast

Well over two hundred years have passed since the Cathedral Basilica was established in St. Augustine. Churches were often the first buildings to go up in newly settled areas, and many were the focal point, some with a steeple so tall it served as a guidepost to the center of town. Churches are important to the foundation of a town, but many are no longer standing, and some have been repurposed, relocated or renewed.

From the start of the Gilded Age in the 1870s to the crash of the stock market in 1929 followed by the Great Depression in the 1930s, Americans saw the Wright Brothers take flight and the *Titanic* sink. Henry Flagler built his Overseas Railroad into Key West a couple of years before America dealt with World War I. Then came the roaring twenties, and land developers, businessmen, new residents and vacationers in automobiles came to the Sunshine State. Florida investors grew wealthy by buying, developing and selling land. And in turn, that resulted in the building of many beautiful and unique churches with stories worth telling.

The glitter of the Gilded Age faded, but during that time, Florida experienced highs and lows along with the rest of the country. Steamboats and riverboats were once filled with winter tourists traveling from Fort George Island south along the St. Johns River, but this mode of travel soon became inconvenient. By the late 1800s, railroads had been constructed throughout the state by companies owned by Henry Flagler and Henry B. Plant. The two Henrys also built lavish hotels near their railroad lines. Rural areas of Florida were slow to adopt new innovations, but resort hotels of the Gilded Age embraced them. On the upside, railroads brought more settlers to growing areas of the state, but the downside meant bypassing small communities. That along with natural disasters and freezing winters in the 1880s caused many settlers to leave once-thriving small villages and communities for city life.

At one time, forty platted acres of the Pine Level community held a courthouse, a jail, two churches, saloons, stores, warehouses, a school, hotels, a restaurant and many homes. Pine Level United Methodist Church was founded shortly after the town was designated the county seat of Manatee County in 1866. Settlers worshipped under a brush arbor, which was most likely a lean-to covered with branches, or in the courthouse until a church could be built in 1884. In 1887, Desoto County was created from a portion of Manatee County, and Pine Level remained the county seat of DeSoto County for eighteen months. But everything changed after the railroad bypassed Pine Level to stop in Arcadia, formerly known as Waldron's and Raulerson's Landing, then Tater Hill Bluff. The area soon slid into decline. Today a remodeled schoolhouse built in the 1900s serves as the church, nestled under an old oak tree, the only remaining building of that once-thriving town. Meanwhile, Arcadia was incorporated in 1886 and became the county seat in 1888. Growth of Arcadia, a wild frontier town, continued following a fire in 1905, after which the city decreed only brick or block structures be built downtown.

Another devastating Florida fire destroyed much of downtown St. Augustine in 1887, including the Cathedral Basilica, which Henry Flagler helped restore. Flagler's interest in church building continued from a marketing standpoint and through a strong spiritual desire. A lot on which Flagler wished to build the Alcazar Hotel in St. Augustine was home to a little wooden church. The proposition Flagler made was to build a new church at another location if the Olivet Church would give up its land. The congregation agreed, and Flagler used the Spanish Renaissance Revival style of architecture for both the Grace United Methodist Church (1887), which he built on the acquired lot, and the Alcazar Hotel. Flagler employed the team of Carrera and Hastings to design the church and the hotel, both of which are made with coquina shell and poured-in-place concrete along with a decorative terra-cotta trim.

Flagler had a hand in building several churches. In 1889, he financed the Memorial Presbyterian Church, also called Flagler Memorial Church, in memory of his daughter, Jenny Louise Benedict. The dome is made of copper and was designed in the Venetian Renaissance style. The Ancient City Baptist Church was organized in 1887, and in 1895, Flagler donated the land to build a church. This Romanesque Revival–style church is made of tan brick with a Norman-style tower.

A notable church in the area is St. Cyprian's Episcopal Church, located in the Lincolnville Historic District. St. Cyprian's Episcopal Church, with its steeply pitched roof and heart pine interior, was established in the late 1880s as a place of worship for former slaves and other African Americans in St. Augustine. When Julia Jackson from the Bahamas moved to St. Augustine about thirty years after the Civil War, she recognized that Episcopal African Americans needed their own place of worship and contacted Bishop Edwin Gardner Weed with her concerns. Bishop Weed responded in 1893, and soon the African American congregation named their new Episcopal church after Saint Cyprian of Carthage. From 1893 until the beginning of the twentieth century, the new congregation met in a variety of temporary facilities. In 1899, Emma White, the wife of a New York stockbroker, donated a lot on the corner of Central Avenue (now Martin Luther King Avenue) and Lovett Street, solicited donations from her friends in Florida and Connecticut, and provided the building plans. In 1900, Bishop Weed proudly consecrated the beautiful St. Cyprian's Episcopal Church.

By the beginning of the twentieth century, Florida had many miles of railroad, and soon the Model T began filling the roadways. Roads and railroads were built to support the growing citrus and cattle industries as transportation throughout the state led to more growth of communities and churches. Land was affordable, so investing in agriculture and cattle-raising brought more opportunities for those wishing to move to the Sunshine State. Other industries were drawn to the area by the abundance of natural resources, such as cedar and pine trees, which led to the development of the pencil industry on Cedar Key and turpentine stills throughout the state. Cigar manufacturing, sponge diving and phosphate mining began to take root. Opportunities offered to settlers led to a growing population and resulted in more financial resources. Society was changing with the introduction of electricity, telephones and indoor plumbing. More churches were being built in newly settled towns and coastal vacation areas to add to the religious and social life of communities.

St. Cyprian's Episcopal Church, St. Augustine, St. Johns County, 1902. *Courtesy of the State Archives of Florida.*

The foundation of many communities in Florida began with the construction of a church. Historic villages scattered across the state and walkable island adventures give a glimpse into the lives of families and the perseverance of early pioneers in the newly acquired territory as it became a capital of tourism. Whether they traveled on foot, on horseback or by horse and cart, along sand trails and sandy roads, forging streams and rivers, they came.

Today many small towns and fishing villages still embrace the Cracker way of life, with the church at the center of community life. Many of these churches have absorbing histories, while others are only a shell of what they once represented. Seeing churches in person or through photographs gives an opportunity to reflect on what life was like for those who came before us. The beauty and grace of each building is only made more lovely by the nature of the place. Churches found in parks and historic villages offer a deeper perspective on life in that area at the time the church was thriving.

As described in chapter 4, the 1887 Beaches Museum Chapel on Jacksonville Beach in Duval County is part of the Beaches Museum and History Park. At one time, the church was known as St. Paul's By-the-Sea, serving the coastal community. Now the Beaches Museum Chapel is a part of a complex of historical buildings including the 1903 Pablo Beach Post Office, the 1900 Mayport East Coast Railway Depot, a railway foreman's house and an 1873 Florida Cracker cabin. The herb, vegetable, perennial, bromeliad, rose and butterfly gardens on the property add to the natural beauty of the area.

The Barberville Pioneer Settlement in Volusia County, featuring local and regional historically significant buildings, started as an idea in 1976, when a group of Volusia County teachers founded the Pioneer Settlement for the Creative Arts Inc. It now features exhibits showcasing the lifestyle of early settlers from the late 1800s to the early 1900s. The popular Fall County Jamboree, established in 1976, features not only folk music but also arts and crafts vendors, a corn boil and a sugar boil, along with living history demonstrations. The property is home to the 1885 Pierson Railroad Depot, the 1926 Astor Bridge Tender's House, the early 1900s Turpentine Commissary Country Store, an 1875 log cabin and the Midway United Methodist Church, in addition to other historic buildings. Midway United Methodist Church, established in 1872, was named Midway because Barberville was halfway between Jacksonville and Tampa on the Methodist circuit. The present structure was built in 1890 and was used by the congregation until 1964. It was moved to the Pioneer Settlement in 1994 and later restored.

The Pioneer Village at Shingle Creek in Kissimmee has a collection of historic structures relocated to the village from different places in Osceola County, and preservation efforts continue. A walk through the Pioneer Village offers an idea of what life was like for early settlers. Aside from the church, the park is home to a post office, schoolhouse, train depot, general store, water tower, blacksmith shop and homes from some of the early

Mary's Chapel, Selby Gardens Historic Spanish Point. The chapel was reconstructed in 1986. *Author's collection.*

Osceola County settlers. At the annual Pioneer Day celebration, volunteers dress in period costumes from the late nineteenth century to portray some of the early residents as well as Seminole Indians, showing how they lived at the time. Today the Pioneer Village Church at Shingle Creek is patterned after the Carpenter Gothic–style 1889 St. John's Episcopal Church, which once stood at the northwest corner of Mitchell Street and Sproule Avenue in downtown Kissimmee. In 1902, it was moved two blocks southeast to the corner of Broadway and Sproul Avenue. In 1961, it was moved to its current site at 1709 N. John Young Parkway and is now called the Chapel. It is the second-oldest building in Osceola County.

Located south of Bartow, Homeland Heritage Park in Polk County is home to historic buildings, featuring an English-style house built in 1900, a single-room log cabin with a wraparound porch, the original 1878 school building with the original school bell and the 1888 Homeland Methodist Church, originally called Bethel Methodist Church. When Homeland Methodist Church closed in the 1970s, it was located about half a mile west of where it stands today. In the 1980s, it was the first building donated and moved to Homeland Heritage Park. The wooden steeple was destroyed by a hurricane and re-created in aluminum on a smaller scale in 1990.

Selby Gardens Historic Spanish Point, a thirty-acre museum in Osprey on Little Sarasota Bay, Sarasota County, is home to archaeological sites thousands of years old and pioneer history dating from the late 1800s. At the park, you will find a 1901 restored home, a reconstructed orange-packing house and Mary's Chapel, built to honor Mary Sherrill, who died five weeks after her arrival to the area. The chapel was originally built around 1894 and reconstructed in 1986 with the original 1895 chapel bell and several stained-glass windows.

Manatee Village Historical Park in Bradenton, Manatee County, was created to preserve and share the heritage of Manatee County's founding period of 1840–1918. The first building donated to the park was the 1887 Manatee Methodist Church, also known as the Old Methodist Church or Old Meeting House. In 1975, the church was moved two blocks to the Manatee Village Historical Park and restored to its original size and configuration. Construction on the church started in 1887 but was not completed until 1889 due to a yellow fever epidemic. The circular stained-glass window or "star of creation" over the pulpit is original to the church. The Manatee burying ground is next door.

Heritage Village in Largo is a living history museum with homes and buildings that reflect the lifestyle of those first settlers living in Pinellas County. One is the Safety Harbor Church, built in 1905 by the congregation in the community of Green Springs, now known as Safety Harbor. When a new sanctuary was built in 1960, the old church was used as Sunday school rooms. The church survived being hit by hurricanes twice before it was moved to the village.

The Pioneer Florida Museum and Village in Dade City, Pasco County, started with land and artifacts donated to the Pasco County Fair Association. Over time, it grew into a twenty-one-acre Pioneer Village located just north of downtown Dade City. Historic buildings include the Trilby Train Depot, a schoolhouse from Lacoochee, a restored two-story home, a log cabin, a general store and a Methodist church. Enterprise Church, also known as the United Methodist Church, was built in 1878 but replaced in 1903. It has been refurbished and features the original floors, ceilings, walls, pews and pulpit. In 1977, the church was moved to the Pioneer Florida Museum and Village.

Remnants of the past can be explored at Cracker Country on the Florida State Fairgrounds in Tampa. Cracker Country is an 1890s living history museum and is home to thirteen original relocated buildings dating from 1870 to 1912. A store, a train depot and rural homes are historically furnished, along with the 1900s church. The church, originally a one-room schoolhouse, was moved to Cracker Country from Gretna just north of Tallahassee. Cracker Country is open to the public during the Florida State Fair and for special events.

The Tallahassee Museum in Leon County features a collection of exhibits including an Old Florida area with a church, schoolhouse and former plantation house. The Bethlehem Missionary Baptist Church, built in 1937, was moved to the grounds as a part of a bicentennial project of Florida A&M University. The Historic Pensacola Village is home to the original Old Christ Church, as mentioned in chapter 2. The village covers over eight acres and features thirty properties, with a dozen open to the public. Today the church serves as a meeting hall and special events venue, including for weddings.

Along a country road in Mount Dora sits a sad-looking old church with boarded-up windows, peeling paint and a sagging steeple. The steps of rubble are being lost among the weeds of this formerly lively house of worship. Other church buildings have survived but have taken on different purposes. In Micanopy and Sopchoppy, there are houses that once were churches. In Windsor, behind a picket fence and wrought iron gates, is a storage shed that once was a church. And a few repurposed churches have been made into museums, such as one in Santa Rosa County. The Historic Bagdad Village Museum is in the former New Providence Missionary Baptist Church. At one time, the church served as a school for African American children, and today it is a part of the Bagdad Village Preservation Association.

In Alachua County, the 1907 Hawthorne Historical Museum and Cultural Center is housed in the former African American New Hope Methodist Church. It was restored mostly by volunteers in 1993, saving the old brick piers and colored glass. The museum is home to a series of paintings by Francis Moore, locally known as Hawthorne's Grandpa Moses, and other artifacts from the town of Hawthorne in Alachua County.

The original Sacred Heart Catholic Church of New Smyrna Beach, built in 1899, is another church that eventually became a museum. When it was moved in 1956, it became Old St. Rita's Colored Mission Church or St. Rita's Catholic Church Mission. In 1969, it was a neighborhood clinic and day care facility. In 1999, it was restored to take on new life as the Mary S. Harrell Black Heritage Museum, which houses a collection of photos, artifacts, oral histories and more that explore race relations in Florida during the twentieth century.

Churches in twentieth-century Florida continued to feature a variety of architectural styles. In 1917, in the Coconut Grove neighborhood of Miami, the impressive Plymouth Congregational Church was built by one man and his assistant. The old Spanish Mission–style church has two bell towers, side arcades and an elaborate front entrance. Spaniard and stonemason Felix Rebom, along with an assistant, used only a hatchet, trowel, plumb line and T square to construct the stone church, according to the church's website.

Plymouth Congregational Church, Miami, Coconut Grove neighborhood, Dade County, circa 1920. *Courtesy of the State Archives of Florida.*

Penney Memorial Church, Green Cove Springs, Clay County, 1926. *Courtesy of the State Archives of Florida.*

The 375-year-old hand-carved front door was brought in from a monastery in the Pyrenees mountains, which border France and Spain.

Some old Florida churches have connections to legendary individuals. Penney Memorial Church in Clay County was built in 1926 by the founder of the J.C. Penney Company, James Cash Penney. His father was a Baptist preacher, and Penney recognized the need for a retirement area for ministers. The church was the first building erected for the Penney Farms retirement community west of Green Cove Springs.

Before he was a world-recognized evangelist, an eighteen-year-old Billy Graham preached his first sermon at Bostwick Baptist Church near Palatka in 1937. He was baptized at Silver Lake near Melrose and came to Tampa in the 1930s to find his calling and use his God-given talents. Graham would paddle across the Hillsborough River to an island and practice his sermons in the peace and tranquility of nature while attending the Florida Bible Institute (now Trinity College of Florida) from 1937 until his graduation in 1940 in Temple Terrace. Graham honed his speaking skills in downtown Tampa at the corner of North Franklin and East Fortune Streets. Today historic signs mark the locations where Graham once spread the Gospel. He was ordained in 1939 at the Lake Swan Peniel Church in Palatka.

Surrounded by a shoreline of both gulf and ocean, the Florida peninsula is dotted with historic lighthouses and overflowing with rivers, streams, lakes and springs. Red clay hills to the central north meet the white sandy beaches of the Gulf Coast and offer an array of beautiful vistas, as majestic oaks and scrubby pines fill the scene and senses with an intoxicating lure that brings people back as visitors and residents. The banks of the spring-fed Suwannee River have an almost forgotten history of small towns that once were a hub of activity and tourism. The Florida Ridge might be considered the backbone of the state as it stretches south to farmland rich with tropical fruits and seasonal vegetables. The Everglades embrace the sugarcane fields, for now. Some of the rustic beauty of the shoreline has been captured by the creation of the Canaveral National Seashore along the East Coast and the Gulf Islands National Seashore in Northwest Florida. Each region offers landscapes as unique as its cultural diversity and ecclesiastical architecture.

Chapter 6

A JOYFUL JOURNEY
FOR TOURISTS AND NATIVES

In 1821, when Florida became a territory, the state was divided into East and West Florida, which became two counties, Escambia to the west and St. Johns to the east. Pensacola was the capital of West Florida and St. Augustine the capital of East Florida. Over two hundred years later, the names and county lines have changed many times. At one time, the area to the south of today's St. Johns County down to Palm Beach County along the East Coast was designated Mosquito County. The name was changed to a more inviting Orange County shortly after Florida became a state. Now there are sixty-seven counties in Florida, and the midway point across North Florida is home to the capitol in Tallahassee.

In 1842, the Armed Occupation Act was passed to encourage settlement in the untamed areas of the state to the south. If pioneers built a house, cultivated 5 acres, brought their guns and ammunition and lived on the land for five years, they were rewarded with 160 acres of land. They came with their guns and families and continued to build towns and communities throughout the state. The Civil War brought destruction to villages and churches, but they would rebuild. Visiting historic villages offers a chance to see what it was like to live in Florida at the time of early settlement. From the top of a lighthouse to the roadways or walkways, take a joyful journey and enjoy the haven that is Florida. As you visit these sacred spots, it helps to keep the spirit of our ancestors burning in your heart. My suggestion is to call ahead for prices and other information.

ANCIENT SITES

First Worship, Then Churches

Listed below are several historic sites, from the oldest to the most recent.

FORT WALTON BEACH TEMPLE MOUND (139 Miracle Strip Parkway SE, Fort Walton Beach) was a center of religious, political and social activity and considered a sacred burial ground starting from around 12,000 BC.

CRYSTAL RIVER ARCHAEOLOGICAL STATE PARK (3400 N Museum Point, Crystal River) features a sixty-one-acre pre-Columbian site with a complex Native American mound. It contains burial mounds, temple or platform mounds and a midden.

PORTAVANT TEMPLE MOUND AT EMERSON POINT PRESERVE (5801 17th St. W, Palmetto) also known as Snead Island Temple Mound, is one of fifteen or more mounds produced by the Safety Harbor culture (AD 900–1725) found in the vicinity of Tampa Bay.

HISTORIC SPANISH POINT (401 N Tamiami Trail, Osprey), just south of Sarasota, is home to prehistoric burial and ceremonial mounds along with pioneer buildings such as Mary's Chapel.

LAKE JACKSON MOUNDS ARCHAEOLOGICAL STATE PARK (3600 Indian Mound Road just north of Tallahassee) was built between AD 1200 and 1500. The site served as a political and religious center for Native American cultures and features six earthen temple mounds.

MISSION SAN LUIS (2100 West Tennessee St., Tallahassee) was the principal village of the Apalachees from the 1500s to the 1700s and the Spaniards' westernmost military, religious and administrative capital.

FLORIDA'S FIRST COAST

A Timeline Tour Explores the Origins of Religions in Florida

Northeast Florida is known as America's First Coast, with many firsts for our country in the St. Augustine area, where the history of Florida churches also began. The lazy and longest river in Florida, the St. Johns River, flows more than three hundred miles north from Indian River County in Central Florida to meet the Atlantic Ocean in Duval County, and its shores are home to many historic river churches. Farther north in Nassau County is Amelia Island and the walkable town of Fernandina Beach. South to New Smyrna Beach and west to Cedar Key, up to the spring-fed Suwannee River, growth continued. Two historic villages can be found in the region. Duval County is home to the Beaches Museum and History Park at Jacksonville Beach, and in Volusia County is the Barberville Pioneer Settlement.

Three historic lighthouses in this region complement the seaside communities they overlook. From the highest point on the island, the Amelia Island Lighthouse stands as the oldest still-operational lighthouse in Florida. Built with recycled bricks from Georgia's Cumberland Island Lighthouse, it was moved in 1839 to the mouth of the St. Mary's River, before Florida became a state. To the south is the Anastasia Lighthouse in St. Augustine at Lighthouse Park. The original wooden lookout was replaced with a stone tower, and in 1823, it was converted into a lighthouse before being lost at sea. The lighthouse there today was built in 1874. The Ponce de Leon Inlet Lighthouse, south of Daytona Beach at the former Mosquito Inlet, now Ponce Inlet, was built in 1887. Once the tallest lighthouse in Florida, it is now a museum.

Duval County: A Florida Landing

In 1562, French Huguenots seeking religious freedom, under the leadership of Jean Ribault, landed near the mouth of the St. Johns River. Giving thanks for a successful voyage and landing, Ribault and company knelt in prayer, possibly the first Protestant prayer by an organized religion in Florida. The next day, they erected a stone column claiming the area for France. Two years later, in 1564, the French returned to build Fort Caroline. The Timucuan Ecological and Historic Preserve in Jacksonville, on Fort Caroline Road, is home to exhibits and information about the Ribault Monument and Fort Caroline. Just a short drive from the Visitor Center along the St. Johns River is the Fort Caroline National Memorial.

RIBAULT MONUMENT

In 1924, the Florida Chapter of the Daughters of the American Revolution wanted to commemorate the 1562 landing of Jean Ribault and highlight the influence of European Protestants in the colonization of Florida, so they had a replica column designed. After being moved several times, the column is now located on St. Johns Bluff as a part of the Fort Caroline National Memorial at the Timucuan Ecological and Historic Preserve.

FORT CAROLINE NATIONAL MEMORIAL

Although the 1564 fort has yet to be found, a fort exhibit is featured with cannons along the walls and a memorial listing the names of colonists. In 1565, the first Anglican service was possibly held on board an English naval ship anchored in the St. Johns River waiting to come ashore at Fort Caroline. It would be two centuries later before Protestants worshiped on land in Florida during the British period from 1763 to 1784.

St. Johns County: Historic St. Augustine

The years from 1565 until 1763 encompass what is considered the first Spanish period in Florida, and it all started in St. Johns County. Centuries of history are on display in St. Augustine to be enjoyed by locals and visitors, with gift shops and restaurants aplenty surrounded by Old World charm. The narrow streets and historical sites entice millions of people to come and catch a glimpse of the past. To the north of the Spanish colonial city, along the A1A Scenic and Historic Coastal Byway, is the 1565 landing site of Pedro Menéndez de Aviles, called Nombre de Dios. The area that is recognized as the site of the nation's first parish Mass and the National Shrine of Our Lady of La Leche Chapel is located there. Heading south once you enter the City Gates of Old St. Augustine, you can stroll down St. George Street past the Cathedral Basilica to the site of Nuestra Señora de la Soledad, located across the street from the Sisters of St. Joseph convent. Along the way you will pass Saint Photios Greek Orthodox National Shrine and Museum and the Trinity Parish Episcopal Church. A walking tour of the area also includes nearby Castillo de San Marcos. The eight sites that follow are listed in chronological order of establishment.

NOMBRE DE DIOS SITE AND CROSS OF CHRISTIANITY

The Nombre de Dios site is where Pedro Menéndez de Avilés landed. When Menéndez named the town St. Augustine, he proclaimed it Nombre de Dios (in the Name of God). The area features a 208-foot stainless steel cross of Christianity erected by the Diocese of St. Augustine and an 11-foot bronze statue of Father Francisco López de Mendoza Grajales. He was the Spanish diocesan priest who created an altar when Menéndez came ashore and then held a high cross and celebrated the nation's first parish Mass. The first mission in the United States to North American Indians was also established at this location. The site is home to the National Shrine of Our Lady of La Leche Chapel, housing the oldest shrine in the United States, Nuestra Señora de la Leche (Our Lady of La Leche).

LA SOLEDAD CHAPEL SITE

Now a parking lot, the site is located south of what today is known as the Plaza de la Constitución and across the street from the Sisters of St. Joseph convent.

CASTILLO DE SAN MARCOS, A.K.A. FORT MARION

Castillo de San Marcos is now a National Monument and part of the National Park Service, located in downtown St. Augustine. Used as a place for worship when the town was under attack, a Catholic chapel with an altar can still be seen inside the fort along the north side.

SAINT PHOTIOS GREEK ORTHODOX NATIONAL SHRINE AND MUSEUM

Built in 1749, the Saint Photios Greek Orthodox National Shrine and Museum on George Street describes the 1777 journey of the Minorcan, Greek, Italian and other refugees walking from the Turnbull Plantation in New Smyrna to St. Augustine to start a new life.

CATHEDRAL BASILICA OF ST. AUGUSTINE

In 1793, the Cathedral of St. Augustine's cornerstone was laid, and the Roman Catholic church was completed in 1797. In 1870, it was upgraded to a cathedral, then raised to the status of a minor basilica by Pope Paul VI in 1976.

The St. Augustine fire of 1887 left only the façade and a portion of the exterior walls of the church. The cathedral was rebuilt with the addition of a six-story bell tower, and the church was extended twelve feet beyond the original north wall. Today the church has been restored to look as it did in the late 1700s. This beautiful cathedral with its eighteenth-century Spanish architecture and a nineteenth-century bell tower still stands as a monument to the dedication and perseverance of our forefathers. The twin Doric columns on either side of the arch entrance welcome parishioners and visitors. Tours are offered, Mass is celebrated and a cathedral gift shop offers religious as well as other items.

TRINITY PARISH EPISCOPAL CHURCH

In 1825, a cornerstone was laid for the Trinity Parish Episcopal Church, which originally faced the plaza opposite the Cathedral Basilica. It was completed in 1831, making it the oldest Protestant church building in Florida and the first in the Gothic Revival style. The spire was added around 1843.

HENRY FLAGLER CHURCHES

Three churches built in the late 1800s with the help of Henry Flagler are within walking distance of one another and only a few blocks west of the Cathedral Basilica. Memorial Presbyterian Church and Ancient City Baptist Church are both on Sevilla Street west of Cordova Street. Memorial Presbyterian Church is at Sevilla Street and Valencia Street, and one block north is Ancient City Baptist at Sevilla Street and Carrera Street. Heading east from there is Grace United Methodist Church at the corner of Carrera Street and Cordova Street.

ST. CYPRIAN'S EPISCOPAL CHURCH

Located at the corner of Central Avenue and Lovett Street, St. Cyprian Episcopal Church is in the Lincolnville Historic District of St. Augustine. The current church was consecrated in 1900.

THE BIG BEND AND THE PANHANDLE

Capital City, Forgotten Coast and Beautiful Beaches

From the capital city to small towns, churches and natural wonders of the area flourish. Traveling through the canopy roads of the capital city to the "Forgotten Coast" of unspoiled beaches in the Panhandle and across the area reveals a natural diversity from rapids to springs. At Big Shoals State Park in White Springs, Hamilton County, there are rapids, trails and rolling hills, while Wakulla Springs State Park features icy cold springs with aquamarine water. From the high bluffs overlooking the Apalachicola River in Liberty County to the gently rolling hills of Leon County and south along the Big Bend Scenic Byway, one can take in the serene beauty of Florida at a much slower pace than on the major highways. From the Old Christ Church in Pensacola to St. John's Episcopal Church in Tallahassee, Florida's church history follows a timeline from settlement to statehood. A downtown Tallahassee walking tour goes past several historic churches, while a trip to the Tallahassee Museum reveals more about Old Florida. Historic towns such as Apalachicola, Madison and Quincy still have the charm of the almost-forgotten small-town community as churches compliment the downtown.

The Apalachicola River not only divides the Panhandle by water but also serves as a boundary between the Central and Eastern time zones. The Panhandle is filled with glorious sylvan sanctuaries and wondrous blue water, which makes a perfect setting for a house of worship, as one longs to stay in its beauty forever. Pines and palmetto, waves and bays and bayous, wind and white sandy beaches with watercolor hues make up the landscape of Northwest Florida. They are all complemented by nearby forests of live oaks, cypress trees and southern magnolias. The area is home to a captivating natural cathedral at Florida Caverns State Park in Marianna, with its stalagmites and stalactites in Jackson County, and an isolated waterfall at Falling Waters State Park in Chipley, Washington County.

A TALLAHASSEE TOUR

Florida is one of a few statehouses that has a chapel—the Heritage Chapel is in the capitol building in downtown Tallahassee. Plaques along the inside walls trace Florida's religious heritage from prehistoric Native Americans to the present day. The chapel walls are made of coquina cast from the beaches between Jacksonville and St. Augustine, and the ceiling and entryway walls are made of tidewater cypress. The font and table are made of keystone from a quarry in South Florida. Three historic churches can be found nearby: the St. John's Episcopal Church, the First Presbyterian Church and Trinity Methodist Church. A short drive away is the Pisgah United Methodist Church just north of Tallahassee in the Centerville community. The Tallahassee Museum is also home to a historic church, Bethlehem Missionary Baptist Church.

ON THE WAY TO PENSACOLA

The small town of Marianna in Jackson County is home to St. Luke's Episcopal Church and Falling Waters State Park. In Altha, Calhoun County, is the Chipola Primitive Baptist Church, and a similar wooden church can be seen near Vernon in Washington County, the Moss Hill Methodist Church. Downtown Pensacola is home to not only Old Christ Church on Seville Square in Historic Pensacola Village but also many other historic churches.

APALACHICOLA

Take a walking tour of downtown Apalachicola to see the Trinity Episcopal Church, along with other churches in the area, and a driving tour to two historic lighthouses on the coast. The St. George Island Lighthouse, originally built in 1852 and rebuilt in 2008, is located at the west end of St. George Island, Franklin County. The 1842 St. Marks Lighthouse in Wakulla County was rebuilt due to erosion and is now part of the St. Marks National Wildlife Refuge.

CENTRAL STATE AND SOUTH FLORIDA

Historic Villages, Lighthouses and Island Walks

Central Florida has a diversity like no other part of the state. From the sponge docks of the Gulf Coast to the rocket gardens of the Space Coast, from Tampa Bay to Titusville and south to the Florida Keys, the area is laden with churches. Famous for its Plant City strawberries, Indian River and other citrus and the original Ybor City Cuban sandwich, Central Florida has blossomed into a tourist mecca. The main attractions are Walt Disney World and Universal Studios, along with a wide array of other theme parks including Sea World, Sarasota Jungle Gardens, Legoland (formerly Cypress

Gardens), Busch Gardens, Gatorland, Marineland and Weeki Wachee with its famous mermaids. Historic villages are located in Osceola, Polk, Hillsborough, Sarasota, Pasco, Pinellas and Manatee Counties.

The golden sandy beaches, marshy Everglades and intriguing Seminole reservations are not the only interesting areas at the end of the state. Lost-looking towns to the north and west that were once thriving communities are still home to historic churches. Rodeos and ranches, orange groves and dairy farms coexist with this tourist mecca. The Celestial Railroad of Palm Beach County and the Overseas Railroad connecting the mainland to Key West are long gone, but remnants of the Gilded Age are still visible in South Florida with the Flagler Museum and the Breakers Hotel in Palm Beach.

Three historic southern Florida lighthouses, constructed in the 1880s, are not far from the many historic hotels in the area. The 1860s Jupiter Inlet Lighthouse is in Palm Beach County. On the southern tip of Key Biscayne in the Bill Baggs Cape Florida State Park is the Cape Florida Lighthouse, and the Key West Lighthouse Museum is in Key West. The walkable downtowns of St. Petersburg, Kissimmee, Sanford and Key West are as different as the stories behind the founding of the churches there.

Historic Villages

Explore the past while enjoying the conveniences of the present.

1800s: Pioneer Village at Shingle Creek, Kissimmee, Osceola County, on Babb Road
- Shingle Creek Church
- One of the earliest settlements in Florida after statehood was in Osceola County at Shingle Creek in Kissimmee, located in an area full of cypress trees, which were used to make shingles.

1888: Homeland Heritage Park, Homeland, Polk County, on Church Avenue
- Homeland Methodist Church
- The original Florida cowman, not cowboy, Jacob Summerlin got his start in Polk County and is buried at the Oak Hill Cemetery in nearby Bartow.

1890s: Cracker Country, Hillsborough County, on Highway 301 North

- Gretna Church
- Cracker Country is located on the Florida State Fairgrounds and is not open to the public daily but is open for special events.

1895: Historic Spanish Point, Osprey, Sarasota County, on North Tamiami Trail

- Mary's Chapel
- The Historic Spanish Point Campus is part of the Marie Selby Botanical Gardens, located in downtown Sarasota.

1903: Pioneer Florida Museum and Village, Dade City, Pasco County, on Pioneer Museum Road

- Enterprise Church
- Dade City is also home to the Church Street Historic District.

1905: Pinellas County Heritage Village, Largo, Pinellas County, on 125th Street North

- Safety Harbor Church
- Another Pinellas County historic church is Andrews Memorial Chapel in nearby Dunedin.

1912: Manatee Village Historical Park, Bradenton, Manatee County, on Manatee Avenue East

- Old Methodist Church
- Several historic churches can be found in nearby downtown Bradenton.

Walking Tour of Key West

The tiny island of Key West, with a shoreline of both the Atlantic Ocean and the Gulf of Mexico, has a remarkable church history. The decommissioned Key West Lighthouse that originally opened in 1848 is now a museum and features more information on old Key West churches.

The 1892 United Methodist Church on Eaton Street was built around the church's older wooden sanctuary. It's also known as the Old Stone Church because it is made from coral rock quarried from the site. When

St. Peter's Episcopal Church, Key West, Monroe County. *Author's collection.*

the new church was completed, the old church was dismantled from the inside and carried out the door.

St. Paul's Episcopal Church on Duval Street is one of the original seven Episcopal churches organized to form a diocese in 1838. The original church was finished in 1841, but the one standing today was built in 1919.

St. Peter's Episcopal Church on Center Street was the first Black Episcopal parish in Florida. Land was purchased by 1887 on Center Street to build a church for African Americans after sharing facilities with St. Paul's Episcopal Church. The original church was damaged by a hurricane in 1909, then destroyed by one in 1910. A new church was built in 1924 in the Gothic Revival style. It was designed by Joseph Hannibal, a Key West native and son of Shadrack Hannibal, a runaway slave.

Cornish Memorial African Methodist Episcopal Zion Church on Whitehead Drive was rebuilt in 1894 and restored in 1964 after fire damage. The foundation for the original 1864 Gothic Revival church was quarried from the site where it stands today. Some of the wood used in the construction of the church is believed to have been salvaged from sailing ships.

The Basilica of St. Mary Star of the Sea on Windsor Lane was built in 1905 in the American Victorian style of architecture. The original wooden

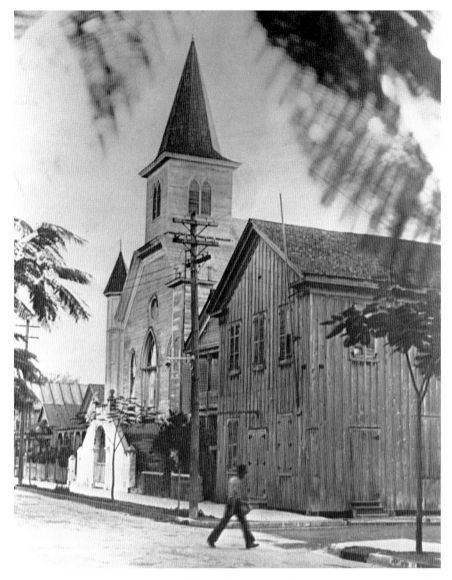

Cornish Memorial AME Zion Church, Key West, Monroe County, circa 1900. *Courtesy of the State Archives of Florida.*

church was destroyed by fire in 1901. The church features two ninety-seven-foot-high towers, with one tower housing the original bell. Louvered shutters at ground level give a warm and inviting feeling to the sanctuary that is highlighted by beautiful colored-glass windows.

GRATITUDE

From the Atlantic Ocean across the state to the Gulf of Mexico and south to the Florida straits, the Sunshine State is characterized by its natural beauty yet complemented by man-made houses of worship. Nature is God's cathedral, but the man-made buildings featured in this book range from beautiful ornate cathedrals to small wooden churches and one Jewish synagogue. Some are so charming they look as if made for a movie set. Others are set in almost-forgotten neighborhoods of historical significance, and some can only be seen in photographs. These historic churches represent our past. Just as historic lighthouses dot the coast and have since the early 1800s, standing against the ravages of heat and hurricanes, churches light the interior.

No matter where you are in the world, the same feeling may overwhelm you. Whether driving through the French countryside or on a train speeding through remote Canadian villages, the church is there, found by the steeple peeking through the treetops, serving as it once did, as a beacon to guide the way for early settlers to nourish both body and soul. It is almost as if the hand of God were leading the way. Imagine walking through the doors of one of these old Florida churches on a Sunday morning. It may feel like coming home, and you just might find going to church brings you joy.

STORIES FROM PAT

There are so many more old Florida churches with stories to tell. Jack and I continue to travel throughout the Sunshine State looking for these historic gems and researching their history. While I have compiled as much information as I could in this book, the story doesn't end with the last chapter, and we will continue to share the glory of our state's history and churches wherever we can. When I told my patriotic brother Patrick Sheffield about *Historic Florida Churches*, he shared with me many of his churchgoing experiences, from one of his first memories of Moss Hill Methodist Church to his time spent in the army. The following are some of the stories from Pat.

MOSS HILL METHODIST CHURCH

On a road named for our great-uncle, the David J. Cook Memorial Highway, sits the Moss Hill Methodist Church, located in the sand hills of Northwest Florida, north of the "World's Most Beautiful Beaches"—or, as it is known to some, the Redneck Rivera. This is one of the first churches I remember seeing. Built by slaves, it was always a scary sight to me and my best friend, Mike Kiser, as we passed it on Sundays on the way to visit our grandparents. We always thought it was haunted, and it might just be. As a child, my father lived within walking distance from this church, in a few different wooden shacks, where he and his family attended services. My great father let me know that for poor folks, back in the 1920s and 1930s, walking distance was as far as you could go and come back the same day. My father stopped attending services there after his father left the family during the middle of the Great Depression. This forced my father to drop out of school at the age of fourteen; he then worked several jobs to support his mother and younger sisters. The doors are open daily at Moss Hill Methodist Church, and services are still conducted, but not weekly.

The Church of Hard Knocks

Army churches and chapels held some of the best services I attended. Stained-glass windows there reflected my reality, soldiers praying—not praying for a war, but praying for their fellow brothers-soldiers in the war. It wasn't until my military service overseas I realized I had taken both churches and the American flag, and what they represented, for granted. This hit home for me in countries that have views which are generally hostile to the American way of life and our values. Whilst in these foreign countries, I never saw a church like the ones I was accustomed to as a child. When I was deployed to combat areas, upon returning to my FOB (Forward Operating Base), I could see the American flag from a distance. Despite having ample U.S. Army firepower at my disposal, I was comforted by the sight of the American flag. Naturally, as a U.S. Army soldier, I do not take the U.S. flag for granted, nor, as a Christian, do I take Christian churches and chapels for granted. Spending my adult years attending U.S. Army chapels, allowed me to go to some of the same churches that President Eisenhower, General Patton (I would think he attended regularly and gave generously to the offering plate, due to his salty use of the English language) and other great Americans attended while in service to their country.

The Sermon Behind the Rock

The best sermon I ever heard was at an open-air church service. Early October, in the year of our Lord 1987, I was in week six of an eight-

week starvation and sleep deprivation course, called the U.S. Army Ranger School. According to Ranger School lore, my Class 13-87 was a part of the last of the hardest classes ever. We had just finished the second of four phases, the mountain phase, and were about halfway into the third phase, the desert phase, at Dugway Proving Grounds in Utah. The next segment would be airborne insertion, into the fourth and final phase in Florida, the swamp/jungle phase. At this juncture, it was still hard to see light at the end of the tunnel, which was graduation and the honor to wear the Ranger tab.

We were constantly under stress by being given only an average of four hours of sleep and one meal per day. We had yet to be given the chance to attend any religious services. This is somewhat due to the fact that there is an extremely limited number of Ranger Tab (Ranger course graduate) chaplains. Ranger chaplains were the only ones allowed to give services to Ranger students. During this desert phase, by day four of a five-day period, I had only gotten two hours of sleep over this five-day span and had not eaten in about twenty hours. What I had eaten prior to that was very little. Since the start of the course, we had been burning about ten thousand calories per day whilst only eating one meal per day of about two thousand calories.

Sergeant First Class (SFC) Yazie, a full-blooded Navaho Indian, was my Ranger instructor at the desert phase. The one and only time I did not fear SFC Yazie was when he asked my platoon, "Anyone want to attend church services for ten minutes?" Initially we thought he was attempting to bait or trick us, until we saw a real U.S. Army Ranger chaplain with him. Thinking we would be punished upon return, only a few Ranger students took SFC Yazie up on this offer. The other choice was to be able to rest and sleep. Despite my body craving sleep, I decided to attend services, because I knew I was struggling to stay mentally focused and maybe some help from God Almighty could aid me in my time of need. Plus, I heard rumors that the chaplain gave out cookies, but these rumors were just that.

My platoon had just finished our reconnaissance mission. It was now 0400 hours (4:00 a.m.). I was one of eight or so Ranger students attending services. We followed the chaplain a few steps away from the other forty plus Ranger students to an area behind a large stone bolder out in the middle of the Utah desert. The temperature that night in October was probably mid-forties. Being malnourished, it felt like it was in the twenties. There we were shivering in our T-shirts and battle dress uniforms, no cool-weather jackets allowed. Following a prayer, the Ranger chaplain preached the best

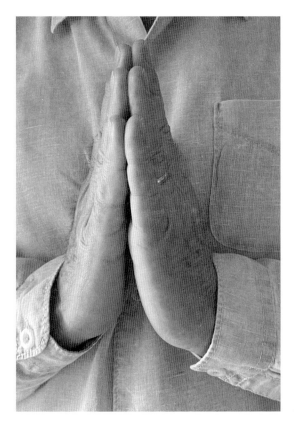

Pat's praying hands. *Courtesy of Hannah Sheffield Abraham.*

six-minute sermon I have ever heard. Being one of the few Ranger-tab-wearing chaplains in the army, he knew he had about two minutes before we students would fall asleep. So he made us stand up to stay awake. He then removed his shirt and started preaching. This caught our attention because I realized things could be worse: I could be colder. The chaplain then spoke of how Jesus calmed his Disciples during troubled times. He basically let us know that Ranger school pales in comparison to how Jesus suffered. We understood the message. Stop feeling sorry for yourselves and go do great things!

THE ARMY CHAPEL

Excluding the Baptist church where I married my great wife Carolyn, the best church I ever entered was in Iraq during the first few months of the

Iraq war. The church was a makeshift U.S. Army chapel. The building we were in had blown-out windows that allowed dust to flow through instead of colored beams of light from stained-glass windows. Due to the burned and missing roof, a camouflage netting was erected overhead in place of a steeple or cross. Empty oil cans and buckets replaced padded pews with backrests. Machine guns and rifles were cradled in soldiers' hands instead of the Holy Bible and song hymnals. A temporary chaplain's alter (travel table) stood in place of a walnut alter. At this chapel I experienced a sad soldier memorial for one of the first IED (improvised explosive device) roadside bomb fatalities in Iraq.

The chaplain was both the preacher and choir director to soldiers. This group of troops could not sing well. I am among those that cannot sing. Back in my hometown at the First Baptist Church of Parker, while attending youth choir practice, the choir director detected a sour note coming out of us kids singing. After a short process of elimination, he figured out it was me and asked me to lower the volume—a lot. At least I was not relegated to just hum the songs like my good sister Joy. This lack of sibling ability to carry a tune was passed down through my late great father's DNA. Back in Iraq, despite the sour and out-of-tune singing, it was music to my ears to hear "Amazing Grace." I believe that song was always the song of choice in a combat environment because there were no hymnals to use and most troops knew at least the first stanza, then they could hum along for the remainder of the lines they didn't know the words to.

BAPTISMAL POOL

As a child, I was quite scared of the baptismal pool that lay boldly behind Brother Taylor as he preached. On baptismal (Sunday) nights, the lights were dimmed in the sanctuary with the baptismal pool lit up, and there was a big, immense-in-stature man, Brother Taylor waving for me to come into the water. The sight of his large body and hands grasping one's face with a cloth and dunking one into water was frightful to me. This, coupled with my friend Chuck telling me that a family of pygmy rattlesnakes were found in the church's vestibule, had me never wanting to get baptized, and for the longest time I thought a vestibule was a vestipool—where one got baptized. Lucky for me, I grew up and overcame my fear and was baptized by big Brother Taylor, at twelve years old. Along with marrying my wonderful wife, it was best thing I ever did.

In comparison, I believe the dirtiest and fastest baptismal pool ever built was in the Middle East, prior to the U.S. Army's departure into hostile territory. On the afternoon prior to crossing the combat line of departure, a unit chaplain had a combat engineer bulldozer scrape out a hole in the desert. A quartermaster unit filled the hole with water. The chaplain gave a short sermon followed by the baptism of soldiers in that dirty water hole. The chaplain baptized soldiers well into the night. The old army saying is so true: "There is never an atheist in a foxhole."

HISTORY PARKS AND MUSEUMS

- Beaches Museum Chapel at Beaches Museum and History Park, a.k.a. St. Paul's By-the-Sea, Jacksonville Beach, Duval County
- Bethlehem Missionary Baptist Church at Tallahassee Museum, Tallahassee, Leon County
- Cracker Country Church at Florida State Fairgrounds Cracker Country, Tampa, Hillsborough County
- Enterprise Church, a.k.a. United Methodist Church, at Pioneer Florida Museum and Village, Dade City, Pasco County
- Homeland Methodist Church, a.k.a. Bethel Methodist Church, at Homeland Heritage Park, Homeland, Polk County
- Manatee Methodist Church, a.k.a. Old Meeting House, at Manatee Village Historical Park, Bradenton, Manatee County
- Mary's Chapel at Selby Gardens Historic Spanish Point, Osprey, Sarasota County
- Midway United Methodist Church at Barberville Pioneer Settlement, Barberville, Volusia County
- New Hope Methodist Church, now Hawthorne Historical Museum and Cultural Center, Hawthorne, Alachua County
- New Providence Missionary Baptist Church, now Historic Bagdad Village Museum, Bagdad, Santa Rosa County
- Pioneer Village Church at Shingle Creek, Kissimmee, Osceola County

- Sacred Heart Catholic Church of New Smyrna Beach, a.k.a. St. Rita's Catholic Church Mission, a.k.a. St. Rita's Colored Mission Church, now Mary S. Harrell Black Heritage Museum, New Smyrna Beach, Volusia County
- Safety Harbor Church at Pinellas County Heritage Village, Largo, Pinellas County

CHURCH BY CHAPTER LIST

Preface

- First Baptist Church of Citra, Marion County
- Citra First United Methodist Church, a.k.a. Citra Methodist Episcopal Church, Marion County
- Spanish Monastery of St. Bernard de Clairvaux, Miami, Miami-Dade County
- The Heritage Chapel at the Florida Capitol, Tallahassee, Leon County

Introduction

- First Baptist Church of Gainesville, Alachua County
- Mikesville Presbyterian Church, Mikesville, Columbia County
- First Presbyterian Church of Eustis, Lake County
- Bethel African Methodist Episcopal Church, Tallahassee, Leon County
- Christ Congregational Church, New Smyrna, Volusia County
- First Methodist Church, Tampa, Hillsborough County

Chapter 1

- Nuestra Señora de la Soledad site, St. Augustine, St. Johns County
- Mission Nombre de Dios site, St. Augustine, St. Johns County
- Chapel of Our Lady of La Leche, St. Augustine, St. Johns County
- Catholic Chapel at Castillo de San Marcos, St. Augustine, St. Johns County
- Photios Greek Orthodox National Shrine and Museum, St. Augustine, St. Johns County
- Cathedral of St. Augustine, a.k.a. Cathedral Basilica of St. Augustine, St. Johns County
- Pigeon Creek Baptist Church, Nassau County

Chapter 2

- Trinity Parish Episcopal Church, St. Augustine, St. Johns County
- Christ Church, a.k.a. Old Christ Church, Pensacola, Escambia County
- St. John's Episcopal Church, Tallahassee, Leon County
- St. Paul's Episcopal Church, Key West, Monroe County
- Christ Church, a.k.a. Trinity Episcopal Church, Apalachicola, Franklin County
- St. John's Episcopal Church, a.k.a. St. John's Cathedral, Jacksonville, Duval County
- St. Mark's Episcopal Church, Palatka, Putnam County
- St. Luke's Episcopal Church, Marianna, Jackson County
- Bethel United Methodist Church, a.k.a. Old Bethel Church, Lake City, Columbia County
- Moss Hill Methodist Church, Vernon, Washington County
- First Presbyterian Church of Fernandina, Fernandina Beach, Nassau County
- Old Philadelphia Presbyterian Church, Quincy, Gadsden County

Chapter 3

- Pigeon Creek Baptist Church, Callahan, Nassau County
- Euchee Valley Presbyterian Church, Argyle, Walton County
- Trinity Methodist Church, Tallahassee, Leon County
- First Presbyterian Church, Tallahassee, Leon County
- Waukeenah Methodist Church, Jefferson County
- Concord Baptist Church, a.k.a. Concord Missionary Baptist Church, Greenville, Jefferson County
- First Presbyterian Church, Monticello, Jefferson County
- Methodist Episcopal Church at Black Creek, a.k.a. Middleburg United Methodist Church, Middleburg, Clay County
- Pisgah Church, Tallahassee, Leon County
- Orange Springs Methodist Episcopal Church, Orange Springs, Marion County

Chapter 4

- Falling Creek United Methodist Church, Lake City, Columbia County
- LaGrange Community Church, Mims, Brevard County
- St. Margaret's Episcopal Church, Hibernia, Clay County
- United Hebrews of Ocala Temple, Ocala, Marion County
- St. Mary's Episcopal Church, Green Cove Springs, Clay County
- Holy Cross Episcopal Church, a.k.a. Church of the Holy Cross of Sanford, Sanford, Seminole County
- All Saints Church, Enterprise, Volusia County
- Episcopal Church of Our Savior, Mandarin, Duval County
- First United Methodist Church, Bagdad, Santa Rosa County
- New Providence Missionary Church, now Bagdad Museum Complex, Bagdad, Santa Rosa County
- St. Mark's Episcopal Church, Cocoa, Brevard County
- St. Luke's Episcopal Church of Courtenay, Merritt Island, Brevard County
- Methodist Church, Mt. Dora, Lake County
- Congregational Church of Mt. Dora, Mt. Dora, Lake County

- St. Mark's Episcopal Church, a.k.a. All Saints Episcopal Church, Fairbanks, Alachua County, Starke, Bradford County
- St. George Episcopal Church, Fort George Island, Duval County
- St Paul's By-the-Sea, a.k.a. Beaches Chapel, Jacksonville Beach, Duvall County
- St. Andrews Episcopal Church, now Old St. Andrew's Event Venue, Jacksonville, Duval County
- St. Peter's Episcopal Church, Fernandina Beach, Nassau County
- Grace Church, Orange Park, Clay County
- St. Paul's Episcopal Church, East Palatka at Federal Point, Putnam County
- Holy Trinity Episcopal Church, Fruitland Park, Lake County
- Christ Episcopal Church, Fort Meade, Polk County
- Wacahoota United Methodist, Williston, Levy County
- Original First Baptist Church, formerly Pioneer Hickstown Baptist Church, Madison, Madison County
- Port Tampa United Methodist Church, Tampa, Hillsborough County
- Sacred Heart Catholic Church, a.k.a. St. Louis Catholic Church, Tampa, Hillsborough County

Chapter 5

- Pine Level United Methodist Church, Pine Level, DeSoto County
- Grace United Methodist Church, St. Augustine, St. Johns County
- Memorial Presbyterian Church, a.k.a. Flagler Memorial Church, St. Augustine, St. Johns County
- Ancient City Baptist Church, St. Augustine, St. Johns County
- St. Cyprian's Episcopal Church, St. Augustine, St. Johns County
- St Paul's By-the-Sea, a.k.a. Beaches Museum Chapel, now a part of Beaches Museum and History Park, Jacksonville Beach, Duvall County
- Midway United Methodist Church, now a part of Barberville Pioneer Settlement, Barberville, Volusia County

- Pioneer Village Church, Pioneer Village at Shingle Creek, Kissimmee, Osceola County
- St. John's Episcopal Chapel, a.k.a. St. John's Episcopal Church, Kissimmee, Osceola County
- Homeland Methodist Church, a.k.a. Bethel Methodist Church, Homeland Heritage Park, Homeland, Polk County
- Mary's Chapel, Selby Gardens Historic Spanish Point, Osprey, Sarasota County
- Old Meeting House, a.k.a. Old Methodist Church, a.k.a. Manatee Methodist Church, Manatee Village Historical Park, Bradenton, Manatee County
- Safety Harbor Church, Heritage Village, Largo, Pinellas County
- Enterprise Church, a.k.a. United Methodist Church, Pioneer Florida Museum and Village, Dade City, Pasco County
- Gretna Church, Cracker Country, Florida State Fairgrounds, Tampa, Hillsborough County
- Bethlehem Missionary Baptist Church, Tallahassee Museum, Leon County
- New Providence Missionary Baptist Church, Historic Bagdad Village Museum, Bagdad, Santa Rosa County
- New Hope Methodist Church, Hawthorne Historical Museum and Cultural Center, Hawthorne, Alachua County
- Sacred Heart Catholic Church, a.k.a. Old St. Rita's Colored Mission Church, a.k.a. St. Rita's Catholic Church Mission, now the Mary S. Harrell Black Heritage Museum, New Smyrna Beach, Volusia County
- Plymouth Congregational Church, Miami, Miami-Dade County
- Penny Memorial Church, Green Cove Springs, Clay County
- Bostwick Baptist Church, Palatka, Putnam County

Chapter 6 (Includes Churches Not Previously Mentioned)

- Chipola Primitive Baptist Church, Altha, Calhoun County
- United Methodist Church, Key West, Monroe County
- St. Paul's Episcopal Church, Key West, Monroe County
- St. Peters Episcopal Church, Key West, Monroe County

- Cornish Memorial AME Zion Church, Key West, Monroe County
- Basilica of St. Mary Star of the Sea, Key West, Monroe County

Afterword

- Moss Hill Methodist Church, Vernon, Washington County

BIBLIOGRAPHY

Alexander, Michael, ed. *Discovering the New World, Based on the Works of Theodore de Bry*. New York: Harper & Row, 1976.

Barbour, George M. *Florida for Tourists, Invalids, and Settlers*. Facsimile reproduction of the 1882 edition. New York: D. Appleton.

Boardsley, Ruth Robbins, and Emma Bates. *Pioneering in the Everglades*. Florida: Island Press, 1973.

Bentley, George R. *The Episcopal Diocese of Florida, 1892–1975*. Gainesville: University Press of Florida, 1989.

Biddle, Margaret Seton Fleming. *Hibernia: The Unreturning Tide*. New York: Vantage Press, 1974.

Bigelow, Lee Eugene. "A Works Progress Administration Church Record for Saint George's Church." State of Florida Archives, 1937.

Blumenson, John J.G. *Identifying American Architecture*. New York: W.W. Norton, 1981.

Brooks, William E., ed. *From Saddlebags to Satellites: A History of Florida Methodism*. Nashville: Parthenon Press, 1969.

Brown, Canter, Jr., and Larry E. Rivers. *For a Great and Grand Purpose: The Beginnings of the AMEZ Church in Florida, 1864–1905*. Gainesville: University Press of Florida, 2004.

Cabrini, Mary-Durkin. *The Cathedral-Basilica of St. Augustine and Its History 1565–2003*. France: Editions du Signe, 2003.

Carlisle, Rodney, and Loretta Carlisle. *Guide to Florida Pioneer Sites: Exploring the Cracker Heritage*. Sarasota, FL: Pineapple Press, 2016.

Cinchett, John V. *Historic Tampa Churches*. Images of America series. Charleston, SC: Arcadia Publishing, 2018.

Clevenger, Toni Moore. *On the Bay—On the Hill: The Story of the First Baptist Church of Pensacola, Florida*. Pensacola, FL: First Baptist Church Pensacola, 1986.

Cody, Aldus M., and Robert S. Kissimmee: *Osceola County: The First 100 Years*. Kissimmee, FL: Osceola County Historical Society, 1987.

Crowley, John G. *Primitive Baptists of the Wiregrass South*. Gainesville: University Press of Florida, 1998.

Cushman, Joseph D., Jr. *A Goodly Heritage: The Episcopal Church in Florida 1821–1892*. Gainesville: University of Florida Press, 1965.

Dibble, Ernest F. "Religion on Florida's Territorial Frontier." *Florida Historical Quarterly* 80, no. 1 (Summer 2001): 1–23. www.jstor.org/stable/30149431.

Dunaway, Marc. *What Is the Orthodox Church? A Brief Overview of Orthodoxy*. Chesterton, IN: Ancient Faith Publishing, 1995.

Dunn, Hampton. "Florida Methodist Church Named for Indian." Phototouring Florida Collection, 1960.

———. "Florida's Oldest Presbyterian church." Digital Collection, Florida Studies Center Publications. Paper 2899. 1960.

———. *J.M. Hayman, Pioneer Baptist Preacher in Frontier Florida*. Paper presented before the Florida Baptist Historical Society, Stetson University, DeLand, Florida.

———. *Yesterday's Tampa*. Miami: E.A. Seemann, 1972.

Eppes, Susan Bradford. *Through Some Eventful Years*. Macon, GA: J.W. Burke, 1926.

Fairbanks, George R. *History of Florida*. A facsimile reproduction of the 1871 edition. Jacksonville, FL: J.B. Lippincott.

———. *The History and Antiquities of the City of St. Augustine, Florida, Founded A.D. 1565*. A facsimile reproduction of the 1858 edition. New York: Charles B. Norton.

———. *The Spaniards in Florida, Comprising the Notable Settlement of the Huguenots in 1564 and the History of Antiquities of St. Augustine, Founded A.D. 1565*. Jacksonville, FL: Columbus Drew, 1868. Available from Project Gutenberg.

Florida Association of the American Institute of Architects, ed. *A Guide to Florida's Historic Architecture*. Gainesville: University of Florida Press, 2017.

Florida Department of State. *Florida's History Through Its Places*. Gainesville: University of Florida Press, 1995.

Frazier, Norma Goolsby. "*Circuit Riding Preachers: They Sowed the Seed.*" *Sunland Tribune* 21 (1995). https://digitalcommons.usf.edu/sunlandtribune/vol21/iss1/6.

Futch, Jana. "Historical Archaeology of the Pine Level Site (8DE14), DeSoto County, Florida." Master's thesis, University of South Florida, 2011. https://digitalcommons.usf.edu/etd/3745/.

Gannon, Michael V. "Altar and Hearth: The Coming of Christianity 1521–1565." *Florida Historical Quarterly* 44, no. 1/2, Quadricentennial Edition (July–October 1965): 17–44. https://www.jstor.org/stable/30147724.

Gannon, Michael. *The Cross in the Sand: The Early Catholic Church in Florida, 1513–1870.* Gainesville: University Press of Florida, 1993.

Geiger, Matthew J. *Mission of Nombre de Dios, Shrine of Our Lady of La Leche, St. Augustine, Florida: A Brief History.* St. Augustine, FL: Shrine Gift Shop, Mission of Nombre de Dios, 2003.

Hardee, Suzanne Davis. *The Golden Age of Amelia Island: The Churches.* Fernandina Beach, FL: Amelia Island Museum of History, Board of Trustees, 1994.

Harris, W.J. *St. Augustine Under Three Flags: Tourist Guide and History.* W.J. Harris, 1918. St. Augustine, FL.

Heard, Phil. *There Came a Man: The Life and Influence of Richard Johnson Mays on the Development of Baptist Works in Florida.* Madison. Florida Baptist Historical Society, 2004. Paper presented to the Florida Baptist Historical Society, April 23, 2004.

Lane, Jack C. "Florida's Carpenter Gothic Churches: Artistic Gems from a Victorian Past." *Florida Historical Quarterly* 91, no. 2 (2012): 248–70.

Lawrence, Charles. "Dunnellon Church Renovating 120-Year-Old Building." *Ocala Star Banner*, July 13, 2013.

Ley, John Cole. *Fifty-Two Years in Florida.* Dallas, TX: M.E. Church, South. A facsimile reproduction of the 1899 edition. Barbee and Smith, Agents.

Lewis, C.S. *Letters to Malcolm: Chiefly on Prayer.* London: Geoffrey Bles, 1964.

Matthews, Janet Snyder. *Edge of Wilderness: A Settlement History of Manatee River and Sarasota Bay.* Tulsa, Oklahoma: Caprine Press, 1983.

Menard, Joyce A. Fletcher. *Windows, Memorials, and More.* College Station, TX: Virtualbookworm.com, 2013.

Miller, Mike. *Florida Carpenter Gothic Churches.* Self-published, 2016.

Paisley, Clifton. *The Red Hills of Florida, 1528–1865.* Tuscaloosa: University of Alabama Press, 1989.

Patillo, Charles E., III. *St. Dunstan's and Johns.* Jacksonville Beach, FL: High-Pitched Hum Publishing, 2008.

Pennington, Edgar Legare. *John Freemen Young, Second Bishop of Florida*. Hartford, CT: Church Missions, 1939. A facsimile reproduction by Leopold Classic Library.

———. "The Episcopal Church in South Florida, 1764–1892." *Historical Magazine of the Protestant Episcopal Church* 7, no. 1 (1938): 3–77. http://www.jstor.org/stable/42968744.

Peppard, Michael. *The World's Oldest Church: Bible, Art and Ritual at Dura-Europos, Syria*. New Haven, CT: Yale University Press, 2016.

Perkins, Frederic Beecher. *Narrative of LeMoyne: An Artist Who Accompanied the French Expedition to Florida Under Laudonniere, 1564*. Boston: J.R. Osgood, 1875.

Pinardi, Norman J. *The Plant Pioneers: The Story of the Reasoner Family, Pioneer Florida Horticulturists and Their Nursery*. Torrington, CT: Rainbow Press, 1980.

Pizzo, Anthony P. *Tampa Town, 1824–1886: The Cracker Village with A Latin Accent*. Tampa, FL: self-published, 1968.

Portier, Michael. "From Pensacola to St. Augustine in 1827: A Journey of the Rt. Rev. Michael Portier." *Florida Historical Quarterly* 26, no. 2 (1947): 135–66. https://www.jstor.org/stable/30138643.

Price, Eugenia. *Diary of a Novel*. New York: Lippincott & Crowell, 1980.

Rast, Jeremiah. *Life Sketches, Striking Incidents and Sermon*. Louisville, KY: Pentecostal Publishing, 1828.

Richardson, Simon Peter. *The Lights and Shadows of Itinerant Life: An Autobiography of Rev. Simon Peter Richardson*. A facsimile reproduction of the 1900 edition, Scholar Select.

Romans, Bernard. *A Concise Natural History of East and West Florida*. A facsimile reproduction of the 1775 edition. Printed for the author, New York.

Stanton, Phoebe B. *The Gothic Revival and American Church Architecture: An Episode in Taste, 1840–1856*. Baltimore, MD: Johns Hopkins Press, 1968.

Stauffer, Carl. *God Willing: A History of St. John's Episcopal Church, 1829–1979*. Tallahassee, FL: St. John's Episcopal Church, 1984.

Stone, Spessard. "Cracker Barrell: Rev. John Wright Hendry." https://sites.rootsweb.com/~crackerbarrel/JWH.html.

———. "Cracker Barrell: Rev. William Penn McEwen." https://freepages.rootsweb.com/~crackerbarrel/genealogy/McEwen1.html.

Stowe, Charles Edward. *Life of Harriet Beecher Stowe, Compiled from Her Letters and Journals by Her Son Charles Edward Stowe*. Cambridge, MA: Riverside Press, 1896. Available from Project Gutenberg.

Tebeau, Charlton W. *The Story of the Chokoloskee Bay Country: With the Reminiscences of Pioneer C.S. Ted Smallwood*. Miami: Florida Flair Books, 2004.

Upjohn, Everard M. *Richard Upjohn, Architect and Churchman.* New York: Columbia University Press, 1939. Reprinted by Da Capo Press, 1968.

Weaver, C. Douglas. *Forward By Faith.* Gainesville, FL: First Baptist Church Gainesville, 2006.

Whitney, John P. *Whitney's Florida Pathfinder.* New York: John Prescott Whitney, 1876. A facsimile reproduction, Scholar Select.

ABOUT THE AUTHOR

Joy Harris is a former history and home economics teacher. She previously worked for the Florida Department of Natural Resources in seafood marketing and for the Florida Poultry Federation. After owning the restaurant Harris and Company and hosting a local TV segment, *The Joy of Homemaking*, Joy worked on two books with her husband: *Jack Harris, Unwrapped!* and *Easy Breezy Florida Cooking*. She is the author of *A Culinary History of Florida*, *Florida Sweets* and *The Florida Cracker Cookbook*, all published by The History Press. Joy has an MS in psychology from Nova Southeastern University and an MS in educational leadership and administration from FSU as well as a BS in home economics education.